M000249742

YOU DON'T HAVE TO DIE TO GO TO HEAVEN

You Don't Have to Die to Go to Heaven

Copyright ©2004 by Derrick Sweet

All rights reserved. No part of this book may be reproduced, stored in a retrieval system or database, or transmitted in any form or by any means, electronic, mechanical, photocopying, recording, or otherwise, without the prior written permission of the publisher.

We acknowledge the financial support of the Government of Canada through the Book Publishing Industry Development Program for our publishing activities.

ISBN: 1-894622-49-9

Published by Warwick Publishing Inc.
161 Frederick Street, Toronto, Ontario M5A 4P3
Canada
www.warwickgp.com

Distributed in Canada by
Canadian Book Network
c/o Georgetown Terminal Warehouses
34 Armstrong Avenue
Georgetown, Ontario L7G 4R9
www.canadianbooknetwork.com

Distributed in the United States by
CDS
193 Edwards Drive
Jackson TN 38301
www.cdsbooks.com

Editor: Jennifer Iveson
Design: Clint Rogerson

Printed and bound in Canada

DERRICK SWEET

YOU DON'T HAVE TO DIE TO GO TO HEAVEN

Warwick Publishing

CONTENTS

I DEDICATE THIS BOOK TO MY BEAUTIFUL WIFE MARSHA. You are living proof that you don't have to die to go to heaven!

ACKNOWLEDGEMENTS

*T*HERE ARE MANY PEOPLE I WOULD LIKE TO RECOGNIZE for their input, support and guidance in the development of this book. First and foremost, I would like to thank Warwick Publishing for its interest in the ideas that this book stands for. I am especially grateful for the sincere enthusiasm of Nick Pitt, of Warwick Publishing, who embraced this project from the beginning. Appreciation goes, as well, to my editor, Jennifer Iveson, for her mastery of the written word, her sunny disposition and her command of the English language.

Thanks also go to my wife Marsha for her willingness to listen and re-listen and re-listen yet again to all the ideas in this book; your feedback, thoughts and enthusiasm continue to keep me moving in the right direction. To my good friends and advisors, Gino Ciavarella, Catherine and Jonas Friel and Gordon Corbett: I am truly blessed to have your friendship and support.

Thank you to Deborah Shannon, Cathleen Fillmore, Pat Gadsden and Michael Holmes from monthlywisdomprogram.com. You have all been true pioneers in this project. Thanks to Jill Hewlett, host and creator of the *Mind, Body, and Spirit* television series, for your continued support and friendship.

A big thank-you goes to my business advisor, website developer and friend Hugh Molyneux, who keeps everything together and always turns any problem into an opportunity. Your attitude is amazing.

To David Aaron, who has always been a true friend and believer: your dedication, enthusiasm and relentless persistence have been a true inspiration. Thank you for your years of commitment to the production of this message.

To Ajay Dhebar and Frank Cianchetti for your ongoing advice: I've always been able to count on your support.

My thanks to the speakers' bureaus across the United States and Canada who continue to support the message of this book by recommending my keynote presentations to their most trusted clients. Thank you to my corporate clients, especially Mike Matthew, Eva Durnford, Lorraine Brown, Carol Truemner and Michelle Jones, for repeatedly inviting me to speak to employees and clients. You are all ambassadors of the powerful message in this book.

And finally to my parents, Betty and Ray Sweet: your support, love and unimaginable belief in me continues to be the octane in my tank, the spring in my step, the passion in my eyes and the fire in my belly!

INTRODUCTION

*F*OR THOUSANDS OF YEARS, HUMANITY has been seeking purpose and meaning—where the blissful feeling of internal peace is experienced for longer than a rare, fleeting moment. Throughout history, philosophers have searched for directions to this place that I like to call "heaven on earth."

The first yogi, Pantanjali, wrote over two thousand years ago: "We search all over the earth for that haunting fragrance which is really exuded from ourselves. We stumble, we hurt ourselves, we endure endless hardships—but we never look in the right place."

This place called heaven is not on any physical map of the universe. Rather, it is a *state of mind* that can be found right here on solid ground. In *Paradise Lost,* first published in 1667, John Milton wrote: "The mind is its own place, and in itself / Can make a heaven of hell, and a hell of heaven." Sadly, today more of us seem to be making a hell of heaven than a heaven of hell.

We have all experienced moments that could be defined as heaven on earth. Maybe you found heaven while enjoying a new and exciting sensation—a new taste, a wonderful aroma, an exhilarating touch. Or perhaps you found heaven on earth in the peaceful feeling experienced watching a sunrise or sunset. But to some, the very idea of finding heaven on earth is more like a fantasy than a reality; it might be more believable, perhaps, if it came in the form of a cure-all little blue pill.

You won't find any prescriptions for pills in this book. You won't find any effortless solutions either. What you will find are thought-provoking ideas with the potential to elevate your consciousness to a level which *could* allow you to drop your self-imposed limitations and enter a brand new realm of possibilities—maybe even a realm called heaven on earth.

Until we find our own heaven on earth, we will wander through our days like lost sheep, with a nagging feeling that something is missing. And as long as this feeling nags at us, there will continue to be a gap between what we intuitively know *could* be and what actually is. The objective of this book is to remind you how to discover, embrace and develop what *could* be. This book was written to close the gap.

According to the Sufis (Islamic mystics), to discover heaven on earth is to "die before you die." At death, Sufis believe, all the secrets of life are revealed, allowing us to discover our true selves. Thus, to "die before you die" is to learn these powerful secrets and harness the wisdom of divine consciousness—to find heaven on earth—now. Put another way, to "die before you die" is to know the truth about life, to see life through the eyes of your higher self. As *Get the Most Out of Life* readers remember, this higher self is the witness to the physical life we live; it is you, as you exist on a higher plane.

Before we get any further, let me say that although I may quote different religious beliefs periodically in this book, this is by no means a "religious" book. For the record, I am not religious. I do not belong to a particular faith, team, church, mosque, tribe or temple. I do, however, believe in God. The God I believe in does not take sides, judge or condemn. The God that I believe in is not some old man in a white robe with a white beard, perched on a cloud in heaven, deciding who gets cancer and who has misery and who gets to work for Donald Trump.

The God I believe in is inside you and me and nature and everything in the world—good and bad. If this makes no sense to you now, after you read this book in its entirety, I hope it makes perfect sense.

All religions, at their core, are paths to a universal truth—to that element we feel is missing in our lives. Lebanese poet Kahlil Gibran (1883–1931) wrote in *The Prophet*:

Say not, "I have found the truth" but rather,
   "I have found a truth."
Say not, "I have found the path to the soul."
   Say rather, "I have met the soul walking
   upon my path."
For the soul walks on all paths.

There are many questions you may be considering as you begin your own spiritual path to truth.

No book, religious or not, has all the answers. I think of life as a mystery to be enjoyed rather than figured out. The information in this book will help you enjoy life; it will help you see through many of the illusions that may have been preventing you from experiencing joy, success, meaning, contribution and bliss.

This is my third book and is a follow-up to *Get the Most Out of Life*, which contained eighty-four practical suggestions for your daily life, to bring you more laughter, happiness, contentment and connection. It was a good place for us to start.

In this book, some of the key concepts of *Get the Most Out of Life* emerge at a deeper level; the underpinning of that practical advice can be found here. Whether you want to achieve more peace of mind or enlightenment, improve relationships or have a greater understanding of the principles for creating real happiness, a good next step is to delve into this book.

As you set sail among the passages ahead, you may catch yourself saying, "I knew that! I just hadn't articulated it." You'll be affirming what you already knew—within your higher self, anyway. We all know that within us lies something almighty—something that knows how to live, what to do and how to find heaven on earth.

It is my hope that as you read the following pages you feel the same rush of anticipation and excitement felt by the great philosophers and explorers of the past as they embarked on their various searches for what *could be*.

Let's begin!

THE HOLY GRAIL

S DESCRIBED IN THE NEW TESTAMENT, JESUS and his disciples drank wine from a cup at the Last Supper. Popularized in the Middle Ages, legends have sprung up about the heavenly power of this cup, known by most as the Holy Grail. In *Indiana Jones and the Last Crusade*, for example, Indiana's father, Henry (played by Sean Connery), searched the world for this cup—but the real search was for much more than that. He was looking for the *answer*. The secrets of life, he was told, would be revealed to anyone in possession of this divine treasure. When father and son had succeeded in locating the grail, Indiana asked his dad what he had found. "Illumination," was Henry's reply.

Illumination—to see clearly the answers to the questions we have been asking for centuries: "How can I find happiness, meaning in my life and a sense of purpose?" Indiana's friend Professor Brodie told him: "The search for the Cup of Christ is the search

"BUT THEY FOR WHOM I AM THE SUPREME GOAL, WHO DO ALL WORK RENOUNCING SELF FOR ME AND MEDITATE ON ME WITH SINGLE-HEARTED DEVOTION, THESE I WILL SWIFTLY RESCUE FROM DEATH'S VAST SEA, FOR THEIR CONSCIOUSNESS HAS ENTERED INTO ME."
—Bhagavad Gita

"OUR NORMAL
WAKING CON-
SCIOUSNESS,
RATIONAL CON-
SCIOUSNESS AS WE
CALL IT, IS BUT
ONE SPECIAL TYPE
OF CONSCIOUS-
NESS, WHILST ALL
ABOUT IT, PARTED
FROM IT BY THE
FILMIEST OF
SCREENS, THERE
LIE POTENTIAL
FORMS OF
CONSCIOUSNESS
ENTIRELY DIFFER-
ENT."
—William James,
American
psychologist

for the Divine in all of us." The Divine can also be called the higher self and when the higher self has been discovered, embraced and developed, the Holy Grail will reveal itself once and for all.

Consider the story of the hundredth monkey, as popularized by Ken Keyes, Jr., in his book by that name. In 1952, Japanese scientists had been studying a species of macaque for about thirty years, on the island of Koshima. To better observe behavior, these scientists scattered sweet potatoes in an open area to lure the monkeys from the dense forest. One day, a scientist noticed that a young monkey had started washing her sweet potato in a nearby stream before she ate it. Before long, her playmates, and their parents, had adopted this trick. While surely exciting for the scientists, there is nothing astounding about these observations. But then scientists noticed something else: macaques on other islands, totally isolated from this group, began washing their sweet potatoes too!

For the monkeys, learning how to wash sweet potatoes before eating them was a kind of evolution in consciousness that began with an individual's idea. With time, monkeys hundreds of miles away were somehow able to tap into this new consciousness. But how? The answer is often disputed, and scientific discourse is not my purpose here. What's important about this story is that it's a great example of the spiritual idea that this book is getting at.

In *Power vs. Force,* David R. Hawkins describes the human mind as a computer terminal connected to a giant database. This "giant database" is called the collective consciousness of all humanity.

According to Hawkins, each individual's consciousness is an expression of the consciousness of all humankind. Collective consciousness, by definition, contains all thoughts that have ever been thought—it is a giant library of ideas. Following this theory, the monkey who first thought of washing her potato had tapped into her species' database to get this idea. And with time, the idea became accessible to the entire species.

Dr. Hawkins concluded that none of us has "original thoughts," but rather tap into this giant database to "borrow" the thoughts that contain the information we are looking for. The only thing a person needs is a full understanding of this concept, and, of course, the ability to ask the right questions of this collective consciousness (otherwise known as the universe).

The ideas behind the collective consciousness are probably not that foreign to you. Think about this: have you ever received a call from a friend you have not seen or spoken to in months, just moments after the person crossed your mind? Have you ever found yourself in a situation where an opportunity found you "out of the blue"? We can all think of many occasions when something in physical reality came into balance with our thoughts. Typically, this kind of thing is dismissed under the catch-all term *coincidence*. But that doesn't really explain these events, does it? It's just an expression we use, like *déjà vu*.

But we know radio waves exist even though we can't see them. We know that electricity is what makes our lights turn on, or our hair stand on end in dry weather.

"THE NOBLEST PLEASURE IS THE JOY OF UNDERSTANDING."
—Leonardo Da Vinci, Italian artist

"THE MOST INCOMPREHENSI-BLE THING ABOUT THE WORLD IS THAT IT IS COM-PREHENSIBLE."
—Albert Einstein, German-born American physicist

Think of our connection to collective consciousness as our channel to the universe. This is what enables us to use our conscious thoughts to manifest our life's desires. Sadly, most people will never learn how to use this marvelous tool consciously. Most of us will limit our earthly experience to what we can *physically* see, touch, smell, taste and hear, and thus never live as fully as we are capable of.

Your mind is a transmitter that can broadcast your feelings, thoughts, problems and desires to the universe. Your mind is also a receiver that can tap into the wealth of consciousness that Dr. Hawkins talked about, just as the macaques in Japan did. This receiver will attract people, ideas and situations that are consistent with your thoughts.

Napoleon Hill (1883–1970), author of one of the best-selling personal development books of all time, *Think and Grow Rich*, wrote:

> Any thought, idea, plan, or purpose which one holds in one's mind attracts a host of its relatives, adds these "relatives" to its own force, and grows until it becomes the dominating, motivating master of the individual in whose mind it has been housed.

Understanding this "blueprint for success" is imperative if you want to attract any kind of abundance into your life. Skeptical? Try this exercise.

Think about a friend or relative that you haven't seen or spoken to for a long time. It may take minutes, hours, days, or even weeks but you will hear from this person. Later in the book, I will introduce the most effective means to tap into collective consciousness, otherwise known as Holy Grail! Before long (if you have an open mind) you will learn how to bring into your life—or *manifest*—all of your heart's desires (the desires of your higher self, that is).

A man is the façade of a temple wherein all wisdom and all good abide. What we commonly call man, the eating, drinking, counting, planting man, does not as we know him represent himself, but misrepresents himself.
>   —Ralph Waldo Emerson (1803–1882)
>   *Essays and English Traits*

"THE GREATER THE KNOWLEDGE, THE GREATER THE DOUBT."
—Johann Wolfgang Von Goethe, German poet

UNITY CONSCIOUSNESS

*H*AVE YOU EVER NOTICED HOW BABIES react to their new world? Babies are truly connected. They have an energy that is calming, peaceful and magnetic to the people around them. Next time you have an opportunity to hold one or even look at one, notice the way he or she looks at you. All babies are born with a unique ability to feel connected to everyone and everything because they naturally practice something called interconnectedness—the purest form of unity consciousness. This practice is natural in the sense that it is biologically necessary, because without eliciting the attention and love of adults, babies will not survive. This is no less true of our higher selves—without unity consciousness, they do not survive.

For the Hindu, the term *namaste* embodies the kind of awareness needed for true unity consciousness. The word comes from Sanskrit and means, "I bow to you." It is accompanied by the gesture of

"Behold, how
good and how
pleasant it is for
brothers to
dwell together
in unity."
—Bible
(Psalms 133:1)

pressing your own hands or fingers together. Namaste is a kind of greeting that, as opposed to the Western handshake, looks inward. Instead of the physical connection of hands touching each other, a spiritual connection is made because there is no such thing as "other." With namaste, I celebrate in you the place where our consciousness is united.

This feeling of oneness can certainly be felt in other ways—between lovers, or parents with their children or a by person observing a sunset or a shooting star.

When we look at photographs of the earth taken from space, it becomes quite clear that we, the earth and its inhabitants, are indeed one. Like the cells of a heavenly body, we are all interconnected. When unity consciousness is achieved, we clearly see that we are all a part of a single living being. By extension, earth is but a cell in an even larger heavenly body called the universe.

Unity consciousness can happen in brief moments, as it often does in my daily travels. The other day, for example, I was driving to an appointment when I noticed a beautiful puppy out for a walk. As I smiled at the puppy, the lady walking it caught my smile and joined right in. All this happened in less than three seconds. For that brief moment, I felt connected to a "stranger" out walking her dog. The feeling of well-being that accompanies unity consciousness is euphoric, peaceful and quite addictive.

When I'm actively practicing unity consciousness, I look at you and see an extension of myself. I also see myself as an extension of you. In this place, the *separate* beings of you and me are transformed into *us*. In this place, I cannot judge you, criticize you or even fear you. Why would I fear myself?

I once heard Ram Dass, one of the most influential spiritual leaders of recent decades, tell the following story. The children of a village asked their spiritual leader—who regularly spoke with God—to please invite God to dinner. The children apparently thought that it would be fun to meet this God person. The prophet was angered by the children's request, saying, "God doesn't do dinner!" (or something to that effect). The next day, when he and God were chatting, God asked, "Why didn't you let me know about my dinner invitation?"

The man reminded God that he doesn't eat. God told him to tell the children to expect him for dinner tomorrow night, which he promptly announced to the village. Well, the villagers were very excited. They all prepared their most delicious dishes. When the food was almost ready, a homeless man appeared, asking for something to eat.

"Go away old man," replied the villagers, "God is coming to dinner."

The homeless man disappeared into the night. An hour went by and God didn't show up. Two hours went by and then three. It was finally agreed that God was not going to come for dinner, and the villagers were upset with their leader.

"You said that God was coming," said one of the children.

The next day, the man met with God and said, "Why didn't you come? I was so humiliated."

God replied, "Oh, but I did show. If you had fed the homeless man, you would have been feeding me."

"ANY UNITY WHICH DOESN'T HAVE ITS ORIGIN IN THE MULTITUDES IS TYRANNY."
—Blaise Pascal, French philosopher

"EVEN THE WEAK
BECOME STRONG
WHEN THEY ARE
UNITED."
—Johann
Friedrich Von
Schiller, German
poet

This simple story gives a powerful lesson: when you see the divinity in others, you see God everywhere. This is what unity consciousness is all about.

The most enlightened people in the world, usually after many years of studying and discussing ancient wisdom, have all come to realize a truth so powerful that it makes heaven on earth possible. What is this truth? We Are One.

This oneness does appear in dramatic ways in our lives, often during or after a major catastrophe. Remember the days and weeks after September 11, 2001. Much of the world united in its effort to heal—we were all one in our grief because we had a collective wound. As a result, there certainly was a lot more kindness, generosity and love in the air, all arising out of compassion.

Here's just one example. One of the immediate effects of the attacks was that all flights were immediately grounded. Dozens of flights landed at the international airport near the town of Gander, Newfoundland, population around 10,000. Having been told what had happened, thousands of tired, shocked and hungry passengers were held up in Gander for three days.

In the months to follow, wonderful stories of compassion and hospitality began to circulate, and were a blessed reprieve from the chaos and fear that 9/11 had caused. The people of Gander had opened their homes to more than 7,000 stranded passengers for three days. They shut down schools, kept bakeries going all night and organized excursions and boat tours to keep people occupied.

These passengers were scared and tired, and this

vulnerability inspired the compassion of people who knew how to help. You see, the two states of mind go hand-in-hand. When we allow ourselves to be vulnerable (like newborn babies), we create an opening for compassion, which is the gateway to unity consciousness.

Time passed, however. Weeks slipped into months and the months faded into years and before long life seemed to be almost back to normal—not innocent, surely, but normal life resumed. And by normal, I mean disconnected. And with this feeling of disconnectedness the illusion of separateness is reborn again. The ego is a worthy foe.

The following exercise will help you consciously see through the eyes of the higher self by practicing unity consciousness. Before I tell you what it is, let me first tell you that I have been practicing it for years. It is one of the most powerful exercises for learning this universal truth. But your lower self (your ego) will deny the truth. Your lower self will tell you this exercise is silly. Don't be fooled. This exercise will change your life. You will never have to read another how-to-build-rapport book again in your life—you will become rapport. Here it is.

Unity Consciousness 101

Choose an hour, one day. For that hour, every time you encounter other human beings, look into their eyes and try to see an extension of you in them, and vice versa. This will be a scary exercise for many. Again, our society promotes the illusion that we are separate from everyone, so this kind of openness

"WE COME TO REASON, NOT TO DOMINATE. WE DO NOT SEEK TO HAVE OUR WAY, BUT TO FIND A COMMON WAY."
—Lyndon B. Johnson, thirty-sixth President of the United States

could feel dangerous. Your ego may feel very threatened; this is quite normal, since we have been misguided for so long. Don't give up. As the Hindu holy book the Bhagavad Gita says, "He, who experiences the unity of life, sees his own Self in all beings, and all beings in his own Self, and looks on everything with an impartial eye."

After practicing this exercise for some time (days or months), you may notice a shift in your consciousness. You may start to see yourself in others without even trying. Later you may begin to see all of humanity in others. Then, you may begin to see God in others. Before long, you may even begin to find God in everything—in a bird's song in the morning, a baby's cry, the sound of the wind and even in a dog's bark. I don't know why it happens, but it does. And it is heaven.

This level of unity consciousness is the equivalent to earning a black belt—in life! When this happens, ill will toward others will vanish from your entire being. You will become peace. You will know the interconnectedness you knew when you were a baby. You will no longer be concerned with being better than your neighbor (ego consciousness). You will, however, be more concerned about being better than you've ever been.

> When a man becomes steadfast in his abstention from harming others, then all living creatures will cease to feel enmity in his presence.
> —Pantanjali (School of Yoga Philosophy ca. 2nd Century B.C.E.)

COMPASSION & EMPATHY

THERE ARE MORE THAN 842 MILLION malnourished people on the planet, according to a 2002 report by the Food and Agriculture Organization of the United Nations. The report also stated that over the last ten years, the richest countries in the world have reduced their financial commitment to this crisis by half, to $8 billion. Yet they have collectively budgeted more than $500 billion for their military.

It would cost less than $21 billion to wipe out world hunger, according to many current estimates. We, in the West, certainly have the resources to put an end to world hunger, thanks to new technologies and better implementation. Despite ongoing work by non-profit organizations, we seem generally to lack the will. As the wealthiest countries in the world ignore the pain and suffering of people in developing countries and spend their money on homeland security and the "terrorist threat," thousands more potential "Osama bin Ladens" are

"WHEN WE COME INTO CONTACT WITH THE OTHER PERSON, OUR THOUGHTS AND ACTIONS SHOULD EXPRESS OUR MIND OF COMPASSION, EVEN IF THAT PERSON SAYS AND DOES THINGS THAT ARE NOT EASY TO ACCEPT. WE PRACTICE IN THIS WAY UNTIL WE SEE CLEARLY THAT OUR LOVE IS NOT CONTINGENT UPON THE OTHER PERSON BEING LOVABLE."
—Thich Nhat Hanh, Buddhist monk

growing up resenting, fearing and hating the West. No one is saying that the solution is simple. But where to begin? That's easy: Empathy.

Throughout history violence, fear and the illusion of separateness have kept humanity's evolution in a spiritual rut. Empathy will allow us to see through the anger, fear and separateness in others. To practice empathy is to understand the following quote from Dr. Helen Shucman's book, *A Course in Miracles*: "All communication is either a loving response or a cry for help."

When others sense your willingness to understand, they are more likely to lay down their arms and find some common ground. Whether you practice empathy with your loved ones, in business, at Parent-Teacher Association meetings or at the United Nations, the goal is always the same: to understand, to listen and to pay attention.

Tolerance and acceptance of others are the offspring of empathy. With empathy at our side we soon realize the insanity of judging, criticizing and condemning others; empathy inspires us to see the suffering of others as our suffering, and their joy as our joy.

You feel what others feel, because you are born interconnected. Doctors report that babies as young as three months old will cry when they see their mother or father crying. This is not a learned emotional response. It's automatic because we are born to feel empathy.

Empathy allows us to come home to a place where no one is a stranger and no one is to be feared, a place where questions like, "What's in it for me?" are replaced by, "What can I do to help?" Suddenly we find ourselves considering how our actions will affect the lives of others, the environment, and future generations. On this day, you will truly see through the eyes of the higher self!

"OUT OF COMPASSION I DESTROY THE DARKNESS OF THEIR IGNORANCE. FROM WITHIN THEM I LIGHT THE LAMP OF WISDOM AND DISPEL ALL DARKNESS FROM THEIR LIVES."
—Bhagavad Gita

"IF THOU WOULDN'T
CONQUER THY
WEAKNESS THOU
MUST NOT GRATIFY
IT."
—William Penn,
founder of
Pennsylvania

THE LOWER SELF

U NDERSTANDING WHY WE SPEND SO MUCH
of our precious earthly existence stressed
out of our minds, fearful of what may
happen tomorrow and feeling that we're missing
something, is the key to getting to the next level in
life. For many people, life truly is an ongoing struggle. Everyone knows intuitively that there must be a
better way to live, but very few of us seem to be taking the right steps to get there.

As *Get the Most Out of Life* readers will remember, life will always be a struggle until we acknowledge and understand our two selves: the lower self
and the higher self. The lower self (also known as
the ego) is located in the mind; it is physical in
nature. The higher self (also known as the spirit) is
your true self.

When our physical bodies perish, so does the
lower self. All that is left is the higher self. Whether
this "leftover" after death is called a soul, a ghost, an
angel or particles of energy is not important. The

"THE FALSE SELF CONSISTS OF EVERYTHING NEGATIVE WITHIN A PERSON. ITS NATURE IS TO BE ENVIOUS, HELPLESS, ANGRY, DESPAIRING, WORRIED, CRITICAL, UNSTABLE, FOOLISH, AND EVERYTHING ELSE AT ENMITY WITH HAPPINESS."
—Vernon Howard, American author

point is that we are something more than the physical collection of brain, bones and blood.

The earthly existence of our lower self, and our failure to tame it, has devastating effects on humanity and the earth. The last hundred years alone have witnessed more mass murders, pain and suffering than perhaps any other time in history, despite our so-called progress. Dr. R.J. Rummel, author of *Power Kills* and a nominee for the Nobel Peace Prize (1996), is a leading expert on the causes and conditions of collective violence in society. According to Dr. Rummel, in the last hundred years more than thirty-five million people have been killed in international and domestic wars, revolutions and violent conflicts.

Here are just some of the examples he cites:

Indonesia: an estimated 600,000 "likely communists" slaughtered in 1965.

Burundi: approximately 100,000 Hutus killed in 1972.

Pakistan: from one to three million Bengalis killed in 1971.

Vietnam: over a million people killed during the conflicts.

The former Soviet Union: from 1918 to 1953, the Soviet government executed, slaughtered, starved, tortured to death or otherwise killed almost forty million of its own people.

China: under Mao Tse-tung, the communist government eliminated an estimated forty-five million Chinese people.

There are really no words to explain this kind of insanity. Dr. Rummel wrote: "Peaceful, nonviolent pursuits and fostering of civil liberties and political rights must be made mankind's highest humanitarian goal."

This is a worthy goal indeed but it will not happen until mankind can identify, understand and make peace with its collective lower self. The slaughtering of millions of mothers, fathers, sons and daughters, no matter what the historical context or who was "in charge" has one theme in common: it happened because too many of us continue to see the world through the eyes of the lower self.

As we have already discussed, your lower self exists to the extent that you see yourself as separate from everyone and everything—including God. It's not that your higher self hasn't been there, trying to communicate with you. It has been there all along, talking to you through that nagging, persistent feeling of emptiness that leaves you knowing that something is missing in your life.

This is why most of us are searching. We don't know exactly what we're searching for; we're just searching. The lower self is ignorant of any higher self and does everything in its power to take us off course as we continue to search for something more. The lower self will tell you, "This is it! It doesn't get any better." However, we know intuitively that there is something more.

The wisdom of the ages has repeatedly warned of the ongoing battle between our lower and higher selves. Those who actually achieve true self-mastery in life (meaning, they've found heaven on earth)

"YOU WILL NEVER FIND PEACE AND HAPPINESS IN ISOLATION, SEPARATED FROM THE OMNIPRESENT GOD. AND YET THIS IS HOW MOST PEOPLE LIVE THEIR LIVES. SUCH LIVES ARE SHALLOW AND WITHOUT FOUNDATION OR DIRECTION, LIKE A RUDDERLESS SHIP FLOUNDERING AT SEA."
—Sai Baba, Indian avatar

"THE 'LETTING GO' (OF THE FALSE SELF ... OR 'AWAKENING') CAN ONLY 'HAPPEN' AS A RESULT OF THE CLEAR UNDERSTANDING OF THE DIFFERENCE BETWEEN WHAT-WE-ARE AND WHAT-WE-APPEAR-TO-BE."
—Ramesh Balsekar, Indian sage

have learned to tame the lower self through understanding and acceptance. They have also discovered, embraced and developed the higher self.

Muslims all over the world participate in Ramadan during the ninth month of the Muslim calendar. It is a celebration of the revelation of the Holy Quran to Muhammad. Since the seventh century C.E., Muslims have fasted from dawn until dusk for the entire month of Ramadan. During this time they are not permitted to eat, smoke, drink or make love. The fast is an internal cleansing, which can be described as bringing awareness to the conflicting forces of the lower and higher selves. Again, the lower self is the ego-based part of you that sees you as a physical being which is separate from God. The lower self is only concerned with satisfying the endless hunger of the ego and the "I." The lower self seeks only to maintain itself through the pleasures of the senses. Ramadan, like many other religious rituals, is one way to feed the higher self, by starving the lower self.

The materialistic society in the West, by its very design, often brings out the lower self in all of us. The lower self is a collector of "stuff." Any kind of material symbol that proves to the world that "I am superior to you" is on the shopping list of the lower self. External wealth is the only wealth the lower self seeks. The entire universe of the lower self consists of the body with *all its senses* and the mind with *all its thoughts*—period. The major difference between our two selves (higher and lower) is that our lower self thinks we "are" our minds, whereas our higher self knows we simply "have" a mind.

The higher self realizes that the mind has thoughts, beliefs, fears and opinions about the world but it does not identify itself with it. The higher self is the witness to all of the goings-on of the mind but identifies itself with a much higher power.

The lower self survives on a diet of lust, greed and praise; it is obsessed with winning the approval of others. Your ongoing challenge (for the rest of your life) is to tame the lower self. How? Vivekananda (1863–1902), the great Hindu spiritual leader, revealed how to tame the lower self when he said:

> Observe the blossoms on the fruit trees. The blossoms vanish of themselves as the fruit grows. So too will the lower self vanish as the divine self grows within you.

As long as we continue to see the world through the eyes of our lower self, we will remain blind and deaf to all of the heaven that surrounds us on a daily basis. The magnificence of a baby's smile will be dismissed as insignificant, the sounds of birds singing in the morning will be heard but seldom listened to. All this, as we continue to yearn for something more.

As you become conscious of your thoughts and actions you will become *mindful*. When you are mindful you will naturally nurture thoughts that support the higher self—pure thoughts of peace, harmony and oneness. Slowly, as you become more mindful, the lower self will be tamed. If you are mindful, disciplined and focused, eventually your lower self will be transformed into the higher self. Like a caterpillar transforming into a butterfly, you

"IT IS A MAN'S OWN MIND, NOT HIS ENEMY OR FOE, THAT LURES HIM TO EVIL WAYS."
—Buddha

"I AM NO LONGER AFRAID OF STORMS, FOR I AM LEARNING TO SAIL MY OWN SHIP."
—Louisa May Alcott, American author

will be free and in harmony with all life. To attain such a goal is possible for all of us!

Transforming the lower self into the higher self is a process that happens over a lifetime. As your consciousness expands, blossoms and bears fruit, more of your higher self will be revealed to you. Your higher self is like a garden without limits on its growth. The only limits you have in your life today are the limits created by the lower self.

LIVING ON PURPOSE

ETTING THE HIGHER SELF TAKE OVER IS NOT easy. There are many obstacles, including the distracting motivations of the lower self. One major key to letting loose the power of the higher self is doing away with chance, luck and coincidence and, instead, living life *on purpose*.

One of the most powerful books written in the last fifty years about purpose is Viktor Frankl's *Man's Search for Meaning*. During World War II, Frankl (1905–1997) spent three years in Auschwitz, Dachau and other concentration camps. During that time, his mother, father, wife and brother were all murdered by Nazis, and he witnessed unspeakable horror and suffering in the Nazi death camps.

This experience, as atrocious as it was, led Frankl to develop a revolutionary approach to psychotherapy, which he called *logotherapy*. Many of Frankl's fellow prisoners were in poor health, and with his medical background, Frankl was able to care for them. This allowed him to find meaning in his life,

"WITHOUT KNOW-
ING WHAT I AM
AND WHY I AM
HERE, LIFE IS
IMPOSSIBLE."
—Leo Tolstoy,
Russian philoso-
pher and author

which was crucial to his survival and psychological well-being.

The basic principle of logotherapy is that people's primary motivational force is their search for meaning. By extension, Frankl believed that the root of our discontent with our lives (our hell on earth) is our inability to find meaning.

Until we define our purpose in life, our constant companion will be—you guessed it— the uneasy feeling that something is missing. As we have already seen, all too often we are under the illusion that this void can be filled with material goodies (like a sports car), cheap thrills (like bungee-jumping) and pleasures of the senses (like extra-marital affairs).

Many people have become lost souls, searching for meaning in meaningless pursuits. We keep hoping that the key to open the door to our happiness will be found through *things* and *thrills*. Others find temporary relief in alcohol, drugs and television. As a culture, we may very well be in a spiritual coma— as evidenced by some of the more popular television shows in North America.

As long as our actions are inconsistent with our values we will remain lost. Any meaning in life will remain in the shadow of "what could be."

Remember, we human beings are pretty simple. To us, happiness means having a connection to life— including a connection to others, to our environment and even to a higher source. And one of the most direct routes to connection can be found through discovering your purpose in life. When we have a purpose that gives our life meaning we naturally think, act and "be" in the realm of the higher self.

So, what is your purpose? If you know, congratulations! You are truly fortunate. If you are close to knowing but don't have your purpose clearly defined or even if you don't have a clue, I'm sure the following exercise will help.

DEFINING YOUR PURPOSE

I've given this exercise a lot of thought. Over the years I've read all kinds of books dedicated to helping people find their purpose, but I have yet to discover "the answer." In writing this chapter and this exercise I wanted to offer you the most precise, simple and powerful formula that has helped me find my own purpose. The following questions are designed to lead you to discover what you are here on this earth to do.

THE QUESTIONS

If you had five minutes left to live,
Who would you call?
What would you say?
What regrets would you have about the way you
   lived your life?
What memories would be the sweetest?
What activities would you miss doing the most?
What dreams would you take to the grave with you?

Our purpose is uncovered when we clearly define our priorities and values in life, which is what this exercise does.

Please, before you read another page of this book, do this exercise! Find a blank piece of paper, or better yet, a journal, and start the exercise. Remember, knowledge isn't power, it's only *potential* power, just

"GREAT MINDS HAVE PURPOSES; OTHERS HAVE WISHES."
—Washington Irving, American author

"EVER MORE PEO-
PLE TODAY HAVE
THE MEANS TO LIVE,
BUT NO MEANING
TO LIVE FOR."
—Victor Frankl,
author of *Man's
Search for Meaning*

like wind, which doesn't produce power until it is harnessed by a windmill or a sail. And if the knowledge is good, when harnessed—that is, when action is taken—it transforms into wisdom.

So many people walk around with a meaningless life. They seem half-asleep, even when they're busy doing things they think are important. This is because they're chasing the wrong things. The way you get meaning into your life is to devote yourself to loving others, devote yourself to your community around you, and devote yourself to creating something that gives you purpose and meaning.

—*Tuesdays with Morrie* by Mitch Albom

AWARENESS

"IT IS OUR LESS
CONSCIOUS
THOUGHTS AND
OUR LESS CON-
SCIOUS ACTIONS
WHICH MAINLY
MOULD OUR LIVES
AND THE LIVES OF
THOSE WHO
SPRING FROM US."
—Samuel Butler,
English poet

*D*ID YOU DO THE EXERCISE IN CHAPTER five? For many of us, those questions are not that easy to answer. Some of them might be answered right away, such as who we would call, and others might really be buried deeply, like our dreams. If this exercise was especially hard for you, don't worry. What you might be missing is *awareness*.

In his book, *Locked in Locked Out*, Dr. Shawn Jenning describes the sheer hell of recovering from a brainstem stroke. Reading this helped me develop a new and sensational awareness of what it means to be able to walk.

Reflecting on his progress at the Stan Cassidy Centre for Rehabilitation in New Brunswick, Canada, he described what it was like to realize that he may never walk again:

I was reflective as we drove home. Life has changed for me—leaving Stan Cassidy gave

41

"THE AIM OF LIFE
IS TO LIVE, AND TO
LIVE MEANS TO BE
AWARE, JOYOUSLY,
DRUNKENLY,
SERENELY, DIVINE-
LY AWARE."
—Henry Miller,
American author

me a final perspective: I will never, ever be the same. I had thought that I would be an agile old fellow, bouncing grandchildren on my knee. I'd have a penchant for plaid, flannel shirts and jeans. I'd be up early, doing odd jobs before breakfast. I'd be canoeing, sailing, and doing manual labor into my seventies. I'd show my grandchildren how to hammer a nail. I'd take them on hikes into the woods. All gone.

Dr. Jennings was a very successful doctor who lived life to the fullest. After living through what many would call hell, Dr. Jennings became aware of how his patients, all those years before the accident, had actually been teachers to him, preparing him for his ordeal:

> I think my patients taught me to laugh more, not to take life so seriously. It's easier to smile than frown, laugh than cry—it is a choice. I thank all my past and present patients for giving me more laughs than tears, more smiles than frowns, and more inner peace. Humor and laughter were the medicines I needed as I lay in my cocoon.

Thanks to his book, I'm now aware of my body in a way I wasn't before. Each time I canoe or go sailing now, I think of Dr. Jennings and thank him for my new awareness of being able to enjoy such pleasurable experiences. He can remind all of us to be aware and not to take one single step for granted.

Awareness of the self isn't everything, though. The key is to develop awareness of unity consciousness. For that, I gained understanding from Christopher Reeve, thanks to his book, *Nothing is Impossible.* Reeve, best known as the face of Superman, was a successful actor who lived life to the fullest. He was enjoying fatherhood, being a husband to his beautiful bride, Dana, and all the other "little things" that we so often take for granted. Then, in one second, his life was turned upside down in a horrific horse-riding accident that left him paralyzed.

Doctors told him he would never walk again, or even breathe without the assistance of a machine. In *Nothing is Impossible,* he describes how he really wanted to die in those early days after his accident. But he also reveals the many discoveries about life he made in the midst of his despair and depression.

> All human beings are equal and equally worthy of loving and being loved. All our relationships must be informed by love, whether inside the family, among friends, or even in the fleeting moments as we pass others on the street. When we sit down at a restaurant, how many of us really pay attention to the waiter? We might listen for a moment while he reads the specials, but could anyone describe him accurately, after dinner? … All it takes is a brief moment of eye contact which acknowledges the equality of another human being. Even that is a loving relationship.

"THE MAN WHO IS AWARE OF HIMSELF IS HENCEFORWARD INDEPENDENT; AND HE IS NEVER BORED, AND LIFE IS ONLY TOO SHORT, AND HE IS STEEPED THROUGH AND THROUGH WITH A PROFOUND YET TEMPERATE HAPPINESS."
—Virginia Woolf, English writer

"IF THE DOORS OF
PERCEPTION WERE
CLEANSED EVERY-
THING WOULD
APPEAR TO MAN AS
IT IS, INFINITE.
FOR MAN HAS
CLOSED HIMSELF
UP, TILL HE SEES
ALL THINGS THRU
CHINKS OF HIS
CAVERN."
—William Blake,
English poet

Today, Reeve is a sought-after speaker who teaches us to develop an awareness of our self-imposed limitations. His paralysis, he reminds us, is physical—real—and even so, he has made amazing strides his doctors never thought possible. Your paralysis could be nothing but an illusion created by your imagination and fueled by fear.

There is nothing but your own fear keeping you from noticing, and appreciating, every step, every wave of your arms, every itch. You probably don't remember the wide-eyed wonder you felt as a baby, but you've surely seen it on the faces of babies you know. Rediscover the awareness you once had, and you will awaken your senses and develop your higher self.

The great Sufi poet and mystic Rumi (1207–1273) captured the essence of awareness when he advised, "Sell your cleverness and purchase bewilderment." I wish everyone would copy those words down and post them where they could see them all the time. Purchase bewilderment. Allow yourself to see what has been there all along!

"HOW MUCH OF
HUMAN LIFE IS
LOST IN WAITING."
—Ralph Waldo
Emerson,
American writer

(7) BEING PRESENT

RE YOU THE KIND OF PERSON WHO is always hurrying from one place to get to another? Are you perpetually focused on a specific task or project that promises happiness only when it's done? Are you spending most of your time trying to achieve a goal that has its reward tucked away in the future? Life becomes very stressful and empty when we spend our time in the present hoping for a better future.

The higher self doesn't aspire to future happiness—it seeks peace and connectedness right now.

And for many people, when is it that they finally stop hurrying? When they are waiting for something, of course. Many of us have decided to wait to be happy, and it's a habit that starts young. Remember when you used to tell yourself, "I can't wait until 3:00 pm when the school bell rings!" as you counted the seconds until freedom? As adults, we count the days to the weekend, or the months to vacation, or the years to retirement.

45

"ONE TODAY IS WORTH TWO TOMORROWS."
—Benjamin Franklin, American inventor, publisher and politician

Always waiting. This state of mind experiences little joy. The only constant in *waiting* is the torment of knowing that this moment is not as good as the moment that is coming in the future. No wonder sales of anxiety-reducing drugs are through the roof!

Now remember when you were a small child and someone gave you something to eat? If you have ever watched a toddler eat an ice cream cone, hypnotized by the sticky sweet mess, you know that kids naturally live in the moment. It's not until later that they begin on the road to deadlines, budgets, anxieties and worry—everything that keeps us from living in the moment.

Marcus Aurelius (121–180 C.E.), a Roman emperor and philosopher heavily influenced by Stoicism, wrote in his famous *Meditations*:

> The present moment is the only thing you can take from anyone, since this is all they really own. No one can lose what they don't own.

His book (a must-read!) is filled with wonderful advice on living in the moment. These words are indeed words to live by, even more so almost two thousand years later. The only place that heaven on earth can be found is right here in the moment—right now.

Now is the time to live! Yes, today! Not tomorrow or when your deadline is met, or when the busy season is over, or when you graduate from school, or when you get a job, or when the kids move out, or when you retire, or when you move to Florida to take up lawn bowling (nothing against lawn bowling). Now.

Tuesdays with Morrie is a wonderful little book about a dying man named Morrie Schwartz. The author, Mitch Albom, beautifully captures Morrie's reflections on living in the moment. There was one sentence in the book that changed my life forever:

> You have to find what's good and true and beautiful in your life now.

Shortly after I read that sentence I quit my job (as a vice-president and senior investment advisor at a large brokerage firm), and began my new career speaking to organizations about all the "little things" we can do on a daily basis to live life to the fullest. Within a year I wrote *Get the Most Out of Life*. You see, I had finally realized that what's "good and true and beautiful" about my life is writing and speaking about how we can be happier and live life to the fullest. Thanks, Morrie!

If there is such a thing as a benefit to having a terminal illness or a debilitating injury, it may be that people seem to suddenly learn to live in the moment. Life becomes crystal clear, as do one's priorities. No need to waste what little time is left fretting about and fearing what isn't going to happen anyway. All the self-imposed complications in life seem to fade away, leaving only this moment. All that's left is the awe, bewilderment and beauty. You see the birds in the park more clearly and hear the sweet sounds they make as if for the first time— every time. Ahhh—what a way to live!

"TODAY IS THE TOMORROW YOU WORRIED ABOUT YESTERDAY."
—Anonymous

47

"BELIEVE THAT
EACH DAY THAT
SHINES ON YOU IS
YOUR LAST."
—Horace, Italian
poet

But we don't live in the moment. The time that we don't waste thinking about what could, should or would happen in the future is spent thinking about events that happened in the past. These "shoulda, woulda, coulda" moments rob you of your present moments just as effectively as worries about the future. Wasting our precious moments on thinking about past events, relationships and decisions can often keep us from taking the necessary action we need to take today, in this moment, to move ahead in all the important areas of a well-balanced life—in relationships, career, finances, as well as physical and emotional development.

You may have heard the line in the Paul Anka song that Frank Sinatra made famous, *My Way*, in which he says he has a few regrets but too few to mention. Paul knows that spending too much time in the past is a total waste of his life. He intuitively understands what all wise people understand—all we really have is this moment! Nothing happens in the past or the future, only the present.

Think about it. What was, is no more. And when the future arrives, it can only arrive in one form—the present. When tomorrow arrives, it's today. In fact, the rest of your life lies in this moment, as does your death. Once you allow yourself to be open to this universal truth (the one that Marcus Aurelius wrote about nearly two thousand years ago) you will no longer try to "get there," because you will begin to realize that there is no *there*, there is only *here*.

Understanding this truth will give you an extraordinary ability to experience life through your higher self. No longer will you put things off until the "right moment" or sit back, hoping things somehow work out for the best. No longer will you dwell on past wrongs or opportunities missed. Your higher self has a healthy sense of urgency to do what needs to be done, today. *Now.*

"THIS INSTANT IS THE ONLY TIME THERE IS."
—Dr. Helen Shucman, *A Course in Miracles*

HOW TO BE PRESENT

"THE SECRET OF HEALTH FOR BOTH MIND AND BODY IS NOT TO MOURN FOR THE PAST, NOT TO WORRY ABOUT THE FUTURE, OR NOT TO ANTICIPATE TROUBLES, BUT TO LIVE IN THE PRESENT MOMENT WISELY AND EARNESTLY."
—Buddha

MANY OF US ARE SO BUSY MEETING deadlines, quotas and some- one else's agenda that we don't even see our lives whizzing by. But, as just discussed, when we focus all our attention on this moment, there is no room for worry, doubt and fear about what should, would or could happen tomorrow. In this state, we are not waiting for the future to improve our lives. We are doing it, now. But the way to focus on the present is not obvious—so, you ask, how exactly is it done?

Like anything, it just takes practice. The follow- ing exercises are good places to start.

Meditation

In chapter one, "The Holy Grail," you learned of a databank of information called our collective con- sciousness. In this "library of libraries," you will find the answers to all your questions, which are not substantially different from the questions Rumi

"Children have neither a past nor a future. Thus they enjoy the present— which seldom happens to us."
—Jean de La Bruyère, French writer

asked more than 800 years ago or Buddha or Confucius' questions of 2,500 years ago. We all may use different words, languages and gestures, but we all want to find answers to the same questions: "How can I find meaning in my life?" or "Where is this place called happiness?" or "What else is there?"

The answer to all these questions can be found through *manifesting*. When we manifest, we attract into our life whatever it is we focus our attention on. In itself, this is nothing new—whether you realize it or not, you have been manifesting all your life. Look around! Everything and everyone in your life is only there because you attracted these people, situations and things by manifesting.

The question is, have you been manifesting heaven or hell? Because most of us are unaware, unconscious or just uninterested, we seldom realize the awesome power of the mind. Instead, we allow it to focus on any random thought, usually triggered by outside stimuli like friends, the media, advertising and the physical environment. This is where meditation comes in.

The act of meditation allows you to focus your thoughts on what you consciously want to manifest. But to do this, you must be present—*in the moment*. You can meditate any time, anywhere. You can even do it in public in such a way that no one even notices. There are many ways to meditate. "Japa" meditation is a form of meditation you can do each morning after you wake up or at night before you sleep. It's a very simple method of meditation to learn; *Get the Most Out of Life* readers will recognize it.

First, sit down in a comfortable position. I recommend having your back erect and legs in a lotus position (cross-legged), but sitting straight in a chair will do just fine. The main thing is to have the back straight. Okay. Now inhale through your nose, slowly and deeply, then exhale slowly through your mouth. On the exhalation, make the sound, "Ahhhh." This is the sound of the divine, and it is what connects you to your higher self.

When you breathe in, expand the area below your ribcage (your diaphragm), not your chest. If you are not sure if you are doing it right, put your hand on your abdomen and imagine that your abdomen is a balloon filling with air. This lets you get a deeper, more relaxing breath. When you exhale through your mouth saying, "Ahhh," slowly contract your abdomen (diaphragm) inward as far as you can.

As you breathe, think about what you want to attract into your life. Perhaps it's a new relationship or a promotion at work—whatever it is, it should be something that fits in with the purpose you defined earlier in this process (see chapter five, "Living on Purpose," for a refresher). Remember, these are not *things* and *thrills* you're after. These are sources of meaning in your life. Visualize whatever it is that you want to enrich your life and help you find heaven on earth. See yourself in your new role at work, for example: your new office, your new desk. Feel the emotions of gratitude, excitement and contentment that you will feel once this promotion is attained. Do this meditation every day. Before long you will begin to actually *feel* the objects of your desire coming into your life.

"THERE IS NO SUCH THING IN ANYONE'S LIFE AS AN UNIMPORTANT DAY."
—Alexander Woollcott, American journalist

"CONFINE YOUR-
SELF TO THE
PRESENT."
—Marcus
Aurelius, Roman
emperor, philoso-
pher

I've been practicing this type of meditation for years. As mentioned earlier, before I started writing books and speaking at conferences, I was a vice-president and senior investment advisor. I had a good job that paid me very well, but it wasn't what I really wanted to do for the rest of my life. Although a student of personal transformation since adolescence, I was very far from living that kind of life. However, through Japa meditation, I turned a dream into a reality. Here's how:

Every day for two years, I practiced Japa meditation with the intent of manifesting this reality. Every day I would see myself in my mind's eye, speaking to large groups of people about the principles of the higher self. And every day, this image seemed more real.

Over these two years, "coincidences" kept occurring that supported this eventual realization. For example, ideas for my first book, *Health Wealthy and Wise,* began coming to me in dreams. Contacts (publishers, printers and editors) were introduced to me through friends. Opportunities to speak to organizations seemed to pop into my existence more and more.

But don't take my word for it; find out for yourself. Find a quiet place in your home where you can retreat on a daily basis. You may want to begin by spending no more than five or ten minutes doing Japa meditation. Gradually you may want to build up your daily meditation to anywhere from thirty to forty-five minutes. Expect to have your mind drift in and out of your meditation periodically. This is normal. Just ignore these distracting thoughts when they pop into your head and go back to meditating. Your thoughts will wander less and less as you go deeper into meditation.

Another type of meditation that you can practice, especially if you're around other people, is called *transcendental* meditation. With this meditation method you simply repeat (out loud or in your mind) a mantra as you inhale slowly through the nose and exhale through either the nose or mouth—I prefer breathing entirely through the nose for this type of meditation. One of the most popular mantras used today around the world is the Sanskrit Buddhist mantra, *Om Mani Padme Hum.* The significance of these words cannot be easily expressed in English but can be loosely translated as bringing oneself closer to God through wisdom and purity.

Transcendental meditation is a great way to relieve stress. For example, I do this a lot when I am stuck in traffic, waiting in a long line, or in the presence of impatient or hostile people. You can even have a "quickie" at a red light! Yes, even thirty seconds is enough to bring you back to the moment and help you re-enter a state of calm.

Silence

Silence can be described as the gateway to awareness. A calm and peaceful mind is an empty mind—empty of all the negativity that keeps you in the realm of ego consciousness. If your mind is full of thoughts, it has no room for awareness. It has often been said that the only language God speaks is silence. Or, as Jelalludin Rumi, a 13th-century Sufi mystic, said, "Silence lets the one behind your eyes talk." Nevertheless, experts estimate that we have anywhere from 15,000 to 60,000 thoughts per day, making true silence a near impossibility.

What is the first thing you do when you come home from work? Do you sit for five minutes and reconnect with your higher self in silence, or do you turn on the television? When you're in your car, do you always have the radio on? You may discover that turning the radio off while driving gives your soul a chance to recharge its batteries through silence. This could be all the boost you need to operate at your highest level.

A heightened sense of awareness is only one of the benefits of spending time in silence on a daily basis. It will also provide the higher self the space to attract the opportunities, people and events that you need to continue to experience your own heaven on earth.

Begin each day with five to thirty minutes of silence. I often enjoy silence after my daily meditation. During this time, try to keep the mind empty of thoughts. You'll find this very difficult. But with time and discipline, you will experience more and more peace during your silence. Soon you will look forward to your silent time. You will notice an inner peace and sense of certainty that can only come from spending time with the divine within you.

Nature

No one knew the power and truth to be found in nature more than American author and naturalist Henry David Thoreau (1817–1862):

I went to the woods because I wished to live deliberately, to front only the essential fact of life, and see if I could not learn what it had to teach, and not, when I came to die, discover that I had not lived. I did not wish to live what was not life, living is so dear: nor did I wish to practice resignation, unless it was quite necessary. I wanted to live deep and suck out all the marrow of life so sturdily and Spartan-like as to put to rout all that was not life, to cut a broad swath and shave close, to drive life into a corner, and reduce it to its lowest terms, and, if it proved to be mean, why then to get the whole and genuine meanness of it, and publish its meanness to the world: or if it were sublime, to know it by experience, and be able to give a true account of it in my next excursion.

The Stoics, who were Greek philosophers dating back to 300 B.C.E., believed that if you live in harmony with nature, you live a contented life. Nature *is* heaven on earth. Nothing else comes close. I bike, canoe and take long walks in the woods every chance I get. At these moments, I always feel closer to God, thanks to the peaceful and nurturing quiet. I can physically feel my soul being renewed and inspired when I'm in nature. This is the reason for moving my office to the Kawartha Lakes region of Ontario, a few hours northeast of Toronto. As I write this book, I am surrounded by acres and acres of beautiful forest, flowers and wildlife.

Have you ever wondered why all the most successful drug and criminal rehabilitation programs are based in a natural setting, where rock climbing, hiking and time to reflect are part of the daily therapy? With time to reflect in a natural environment, the answers to many of our problems seem to appear out of nowhere. I get some of my best ideas for my talks and books while in nature.

To sum up, meditation, silence and time spent in nature are three ways to practice living in the moment, not the future or the past. In essence, they are all ways to give voice to your intuition—your "gut feeling"—which is your inner guidance system. Listen closely to it, and it will tell you which way to go in life, what does or doesn't make sense and when to take action or wait for the right moment.

My mentor, Wayne Dyer, says, "If your prayer is you talking to God, then intuition is God talking to you." Are you curious to know what God has to say to you? Today's as good a day as any to take a walk in the woods!

"WHATEVER I AM
OFFERED IN DEVO-
TION WITH A PURE
HEART—A LEAF, A
FLOWER, FRUIT, OR
WATER—I ACCEPT
WITH JOY."
—Bhagavad Gita

GRATITUDE

BE GRATEFUL FOR YOUR YOUTH BEFORE IT
fades away
And cherish your old age which lasts for
but a day
Be grateful for your health before its expiration
And freely spend your wealth before its termination
Be grateful for your problems before they're all
but solved
And celebrate your life before death's certain call
Be grateful for your love before her fate is met
Take time to watch the sun before it leaves to set
Be grateful for *this* moment and know its power too
Then you'll know that heaven is really up to you
—Derrick Sweet

We create heaven in our life by building a strong
foundation. One of the most important ingredients
in this foundation is gratitude. Bliss, joy and enthusiasm are all by-products of gratitude. When I was
a financial advisor for a large investment firm, I had

59

"ONE UNGRATEFUL
PERSON, DOES AN
INJURY TO ALL
NEEDY PEOPLE."
—Publilius Syrus,
Roman author

the opportunity to meet and work with many people who were wealthy—financially, anyway.

I would often see three to four clients per day in my office. The super-rich clients (with a net worth of several million dollars) were really interesting. Some of them were pretty happy but many more would complain about not having enough money. They often felt compelled to "keep up" with their peer group—other rich people. Often these clients had a home in the country, one in the city, and a condo in Florida. Usually, they had just enough money to pay the bills.

Greed can motivate us to accumulate financial wealth, but as long as we practice greed we will experience life with a poverty consciousness. Poverty consciousness is consciousness of not having enough, and does not just refer to material possessions. It can include not having enough love, peace of mind, free time, health, laughter, connection with others or connection with nature. The list is huge. Most people who suffer from poverty consciousness don't even know they have it. But there is a cure.

The cure for poverty consciousness is simple: gratitude. Being grateful in life takes hard work initially, for some people. Others just seem to naturally have this heavenly disposition. And it is heaven to be around people who seem to feel lucky to be here, in this moment, doing whatever they are doing.

Again, you are saying, this sounds great, but how is it done? Luckily, there is a really simple place to start. You begin to feel gratitude by practicing generosity; the act of being generous to others creates gratitude. There are three basic types of generosity, each one creating a different level of gratitude: basic, anonymous and heavenly generosity. Let's look at all three.

1. Basic Generosity:

This type of generosity is the most common. If we offer someone money, time or a favor of some kind, it is considered an act of basic generosity. An example would be if I saw you in a restaurant and said something like, "Hey friend, I would like to buy you breakfast." This type of generosity, although nice, is merely a transaction that feeds my ego. For my good deed, I am thanked, complimented and honored; I look good. You may even tell a few people what a nice person I am, and, you will most likely repay the favor the next time we meet. Lama Yeshe Losal, a Tibetan Buddhist monk and teacher, says, "Expecting something for your help is like giving a spoonful of honey but mixing it with poison."

2. Anonymous Generosity:

This type of generosity comes from a higher consciousness and is less concerned with feeding the ego. In the restaurant example, I may call your server over and ask to have your bill included with mine, without telling you. I may instruct the server to only tell you that your breakfast is free today. This means that my ego isn't directly fed by your thanks and warmth. But there is still a kind of ego boost, because I know—and the server knows—that I am a "good guy." Each time I see you afterward, I will relish the memory of having done

"THERE IS A CALMNESS TO A LIFE LIVED IN GRATITUDE, A QUIET JOY."
—Ralph H. Blum, American author

"GOD HAS TWO
DWELLINGS; ONE
IN HEAVEN, AND
THE OTHER IN A
MEEK AND THANK-
FUL HEART."
—Izaak Walton,
British writer

something nice for you, feeding my ego a little more each time.

3. Heavenly Generosity:

This type of generosity comes from the purest type of consciousness and has no ego involved at all. This type of generosity is focused on the act of generosity alone because the reward is to be found simply in the act of being generous. This type of consciousness connects you directly to your higher self, leading to a pleasantly overwhelming sense of well-being. How does one practice this magnificent type of bliss?

Well, let's say I was walking down the street and I noticed a car with an expired meter. The generous act of depositing a coin or two in this stranger's parking meter is practicing heavenly generosity. This type of generosity is not between you and the owner of the car, it's between you and your connection to life. Each act of heavenly generosity creates a deeper, richer connection to life, to your higher self and to heaven!

This type of generosity is perhaps the toughest, only because we don't always notice the opportunities when they arise. But, of course, when we're living in the moment—not distracted by our constant worries—it's a lot easier to notice the empty parking meters around us.

The benefits of practicing generosity are too numerous to list in this book. You will find this type of consciousness very addictive. Why? Well, there is a biological explanation. Each time you practice generosity, the body releases serotonin, which, with structural similarities to LSD, is the body's natural feel-good drug. Not only that, it reduces blood pressure, aids in digestion, lowers cholesterol and nourishes the soul!

The miracle is not to walk on water, the miracle is that we can walk on Earth.
—Thich Nhat Hanh,
Buddhist monk and author

"GRATITUDE IS THE FAIREST BLOSSOM WHICH SPRINGS FROM THE SOUL."
—Henry Ward Beecher, American preacher

CHOICES

E VERYTHING CAN BE TAKEN FROM A MAN BUT one thing: the last of human freedoms—to choose one's attitude in any given set of circumstances, to choose one's own way.

—Victor Frankl

"MAN IS MADE OR UNMADE BY HIMSELF. BY THE RIGHT CHOICE HE ASCENDS. AS A BEING OF POWER, INTELLIGENCE, AND LOVE, AND THE LORD OF HIS OWN THOUGHTS, HE HOLDS THE KEY TO EVERY SITUATION."
—James Allen, American author

Over the course of an average week you may make tens of thousands of choices about what to eat, how to feel, what to say, what to watch on television, what to listen to, how you react to various stimuli in your environment, and countless others. Most of the choices you make on a daily basis you make out of habit, without much thought to their long-term consequences. But here's the thing: every single choice you make has an impact on who you become. The long-term impact of your cumulative choices can be explained in a word: *karma.*

Basically, karma is cause and effect. For example, the choice of words you use on a day-to-day basis has a rippling effect on your life. Your emotions,

"YOU AND I ARE ESSENTIALLY INFINITE CHOICE-MAKERS. IN EVERY MOMENT OF OUR EXISTENCE, WE ARE IN THAT FIELD OF ALL POSSIBILITIES WHERE WE HAVE ACCESS TO AN INFINITY OF CHOICES."
—Deepak Chopra, Indian-born American author and lecturer

your energy level, and every action you take are influenced by what words you use to paint the picture of your world. Put another way, the quality of the words you use to describe your life has the potential to create a living heaven or hell.

Think of your mind as a garden. As such, it can produce an unlimited variety of plants that either nourish or contaminate the soul. In this garden, the seeds we plant are the words we use, and the soil we plant them in is the subconscious mind. Think about it. When asked a simple question like "How are you doing?" many people use words that produce weeds rather than roses. "Can't complain," or "Not bad," or "Is it Friday yet?"

Notice how you feel the next time you hear someone choose to use a disempowering word to describe how he or she feels. Or better yet try it now. Go ahead, ask yourself how you're feeling. Try answering the question the first time with the common, habitual response, "Can't complain." Notice how that feels. Repeat the exercise enough to really feel how the words "Not bad" impact negatively on your mood.

Now, try the exercise again but this time take it up a notch. Try responding with a slightly more positive answer like, "Great!" Again, try it a couple of times and notice how you feel. You'll probably notice your mood elevate a few notches to a happier place.

Okay, now it's time to have some fun. "How are you feeling?" This time, answer the question with an extremely jubilant, euphoric, enthusiastic, just-won-the-lottery, life-doesn't-get-any-better-than-this kind of answer. For example, try, "Fantastic!" or "Grrreat!" or "I feel terrific." Again, do this exercise a few times to notice the difference. Next, alternate between the worst answer and the best answer. The negative or positive impact of our choice words on our mood becomes obvious after repeating this exercise. It is an excellent reminder for us to choose the right words for the mood we want to experience.

Going back to the biological explanation for a moment, studies have indicated that the simple act of smiling (meaning, physically forming your face in the shape of a smile, whether or not it is in response to something funny) actually boosts the serotonin levels in your brain, and thus changes your mood. Similarly, your brain has an emotional memory of words like "Grrreat!" that causes a boost in mood.

Choosing words that have an inspirational or uplifting effect on your state of mind isn't being a "Pollyanna," nor is it being insincere; rather, it is acknowledging and benefiting from the connection between words and emotions. Your ongoing challenge, to truly benefit from this simple technique, is to be aware of your every thought and to be mindful of choosing the wrong words.

This may be difficult when you are in stressful situations like getting stuck in a traffic jam when you are running late. Think of such moments as tests. They are tests of your awareness that every word you choose is directly linked to the emotion you feel. And every emotion is linked to every action you take. So, every action always has and always will define your life.

"THE FIRST THING I DO IN THE MORNING IS TO MAKE MY BED AND WHILE I AM MAKING UP MY BED I AM MAKING UP MY MIND AS TO WHAT KIND OF A DAY I AM GOING TO HAVE."
—Robert Frost, American poet

"THERE ARE TWO
PRIMARY CHOICES
IN LIFE: TO ACCEPT
CONDITIONS AS
THEY EXIST, OR
ACCEPT THE
RESPONSIBILITY
FOR CHANGING
THEM."
—Dennis Waitley,
American author

Think about that last paragraph. Perhaps you could even read it again. Don't be in too much of a hurry to get to the next page, or finish this chapter. Remember, you and I both want you to get the same thing from this book: an evolved perspective of who you are and what you're capable of. At the core of this powerful realization is the truth of these sentences. Did you read them over yet?

It will be all too easy, when stuck in traffic, to habitually choose words that produce emotions, and therefore actions, that are inconsistent with the kind of scenario you want to produce. When you catch yourself in these moments, I suggest that you ask yourself how your higher self might react in this kind of circumstance.

I live about three and a half hours away from the nearest major airport and find myself in traffic jams quite regularly as I try to make it to the airport in time to catch my flight. I have two strategies to keep me "aware" of the words I choose to use when, for example, a driver cuts in front of me, causing me to slam on the brakes. The first strategy I choose is listening to calming music. This is the only time I listen to classical music. I love classical music but only in traffic! I find that the soothing sounds of the violin or flute, so prevalent in classical music, put me in a frame of mind to be more proactive than reactive.

When we are reactive, our response to stress is often influenced by our ego. Our ego often motivates us to criticize, judge or maybe scream our heads off at another driver. We've all had moments like this. Obviously, these kinds of angry responses have a terrible effect on your mood; they can ruin your day. When we experience anger, anxiety or stress, the brain releases a hormone called cortisol. Not only is having too much cortisol in your bloodstream bad for your mood, it can also do damage to your heart, thanks to increased blood pressure.

In May 2000, a public-health expert named Dr. Janice Williams published a report in *Circulation* that showed that people who are easily angered are more likely to have a heart attack than those who react to stress in a more positive manner. In the study, scientists asked nearly 13,000 people how they respond in stressful situations. For example, the subjects were asked if they agreed or disagreed with statements like, "I get angry when I am slowed down by other people's mistakes," and "When I get frustrated I feel like hitting someone."

Over the six years of the study, participants who described having the most angry reactions also had the greatest risk of suffering a heart attack or other sudden cardiac death. The angriest group was three times more likely to have an acute or fatal heart attack and twice as likely to develop heart disease than the least angry group. So the next time someone cuts you off in traffic or gets in front of you at the grocery store or annoys you in any other manner, remember that the response you choose has an effect on your physical health, not to mention your emotional health. Again, developing an acute sense of awareness is half the battle!

The words you use have an even greater impact when you consider the ones you use inside your head. Whether you realize it or not, you have been having a dialogue with yourself ever since child-

"ONE'S PHILOSOPHY IS NOT BEST EXPRESSED IN WORDS; IT IS EXPRESSED IN THE CHOICES ONE MAKES. IN THE LONG RUN, WE SHAPE OUR LIVES AND WE SHAPE OURSELVES. THE PROCESS NEVER ENDS UNTIL WE DIE. AND, THE CHOICES WE MAKE ARE ULTIMATELY OUR OWN RESPONSIBILITY."
—Eleanor Roosevelt, American First Lady, journalist

"YOU ARE EVERY-
THING THAT IS,
YOUR THOUGHTS,
YOUR LIFE, YOUR
DREAMS COME
TRUE. YOU ARE
EVERYTHING YOU
CHOOSE TO BE.
YOU ARE AS UNLIM-
ITED AS THE END-
LESS UNIVERSE."
—Shad
Helmstetter,
American author

hood. The words you choose (consciously or unconsciously) when communicating with yourself have a profound impact on your sense of well-being. What kinds of words do you choose? How many times do you choose to say to yourself, "I'm never going to lose this weight," or "I am never going to get out of debt," or "I will never make enough money to buy my dream home"?

Most people practice this type of self-destruction without even realizing it. No one really wants to create a living hell by choosing words with such negative energy but, like so many of our self-defeating behaviors, it just becomes a habit.

Here's another common example of self-defeat. What kinds of food do you choose to eat? Are you choosing convenience over nutrition? Have you chosen not to consider the long-term consequences of choosing convenience over health every day? Again, we all want to create heaven on earth in our lives but to do it, we must become conscious of the impact of every single choice we make.

This type of awareness is not commonly practiced, thanks to the mentality of, "Hurry up and finish what we're doing, now, so we can hurry up and do whatever we have to do next."

And so life goes on and we end up where we end up, all because we choose not to think about the consequences of our choices. Again, for most people, this happens unconsciously, most of the time. But once we begin to choose to think about the consequences of our choices, we begin to make more intelligent decisions. When we consciously make intelligent decisions that are consistent with the intentions of our higher self, we begin to realize the process involved in creating the state of mind called heaven on earth.

Exercise

Take inventory of your choices. Write a list of all the choices you have made in your life that have had a positive impact on you. Going to university, quitting smoking and getting married to your soul-mate may be some of the positive choices you have made. Beside each item, describe the positive impact each choice has had on your life. Then list some of the positive choices you are making now, on a daily basis, that will continue to have a positive impact on your life.

An alternative approach to the exercise is to choose one positive decision and really examine its impact from all angles. For me, choosing to go back to high school and eventually attending Johnson State College in Vermont was one of the most important decisions I have ever made. Being a high school drop-out was very depressing and left me with very few options. The list of positive effects of going back to school is too long to print in its entirety here. Certainly the friendships I made during my four years in college have had a positive and lasting impact. As a shy young man, developing social skills and confidence as a resident assistant, ski instructor, spring-break organizer and ski-pass sales representative were instrumental in my success in my first career, in business.

Today, I continue to be conscious of the long-term consequences of all the major decisions I make

"IT IS ALWAYS YOUR NEXT MOVE."
—Napoleon Hill, American author and lecturer

in my life. Choosing to retire at the age of thirty-eight from a lucrative career to become a writer and speaker seemed like a crazy idea to many of my colleagues in the investment business.

"You'll make no money, you idiot. Don't be stupid," my manager pleaded.

At the time of this writing I am in my third year of being a writer and speaker. I have more free time now to hike, cross-country ski, mountain bike and be with my wife and family. My first two books are in demand all over the world and I'm speaking at the annual conferences of some of the most progressive companies in the world!

Although I did have a few sleepless nights during the first few months of this career move, I have never been happier, nor have I felt more connected to my purpose in life. I'm doing what I always wanted to do and have never felt more alive.

After you have examined your life in a similar way, begin to take a look at the choices that have had a negative impact on your life. Write a list of all the negative choices you continue to make today, on a daily basis. These are the choices that conflict directly with the aspirations of your higher self. Beside each negative choice, write the long-term consequences of continuing to make these choices. Choosing to stay up late and rely on coffee to keep you going every day of your life, for example, will likely have negative long-term consequences directly (your increased stress could lead to a heart condition later in life) and indirectly (your partner could grow tired of your grumpiness and exhaustion). Then, write the positive consequences of retiring these kinds of choices. A healthier lifestyle could lead to all kinds of positive results!

For some of your tougher habits, you might need an action plan to replace your self-defeating choices. Write out the steps it will take to move closer to the aspirations of your higher self, and start your journey.

"THE CONCEPT OF
BOREDOM ENTAILS
AN INABILITY TO
USE UP PRESENT
MOMENTS IN A
PERSONALLY
FULFILLING WAY."
—Wayne Dyer,
American author
and writer

BELIEFS & EXPECTATIONS

*M*OST OF THE LIMITATIONS IN your life originate from a misunderstanding you have about the world. And this misunderstanding is created by your beliefs.

There was a time when people thought they would fall off the edge of the world if they walked far enough. A hundred years ago, according to the *British Medical Journal,* doctors believed that if a menstruating woman touched a ham, it would turn rancid. Clearly, these beliefs affected, in big and small ways, how people viewed the world.

Similarly, your dominant beliefs about the world play a vital role in whether you experience heaven or hell on earth.

These beliefs have been influenced by all kinds of variables: family, schooling, religion, culture, the media, to name a few. Your every thought, emotion and action is influenced by your dominant beliefs, as is your approach to culture, religion, fashion,

75

"In eternity there is indeed something true and sublime. But all these times and places and occasions are now and here. God himself culminates in the present moment and will never be more divine in the lapse of the ages. Time is but a stream I go a-fishing in. I drink at it, but when I drink I see the sandy bottom and detect how shallow it is. Its thin current slides away but eternity remains."

—Henry David Thoreau, American poet

politics, manners, sports, money, love and pretty much anything else. The belief that "blondes have more fun" may influence you to dye your hair blonde. The belief that healthy people don't eat fried food may steer you away from french fries. Your belief that a happy marriage will make you happy in other areas of your life may motivate you to choose to work things out while others in similar circumstances choose to file for divorce.

Whether you realize it or not, each of us has an army of beliefs pulling us in different directions. Some of your core beliefs support thoughts, feelings and actions that nurture your higher self, while others feed the self-defeating ways of the lower self. When we are mindful of the karmic price we pay for our beliefs, we are much more likely to take inventory of our beliefs. What are your negative beliefs? Any belief that weakens you in any way must be viewed as negative.

As you take inventory, the voice of the lower self may try to justify these toxic beliefs. For example, if you believe that men can't be trusted, your higher self will tell you to include this among your negative or limiting beliefs. But the lower self, concerned for its dominance over you, may lead you to think of the men who have lied, cheated or disappointed you. It may want you to keep this belief because it has been "proven" to you over and over. But this so-called proof is nothing of the sort; the fact is that the belief has become a kind of self-fulfilling prophecy. Why? Because the human mind seeks congruency. It seeks a reality that "matches up" with its beliefs.

Having a core belief that men can't be trusted—no matter where the belief came from—has caused you to subconsciously support this belief through your ongoing thoughts, feelings and actions. In other words, you have sought out untrustworthy men because they are what you expect. Your lower self does not like to be "wrong" so it seeks out an environment that supports the beliefs, regardless of whether these beliefs are true or, more importantly, helpful to you.

In this way, your core beliefs heavily influence your expectations. If you believe that without a university degree you will live in poverty, this belief will lead you to expect a lower income and may even lead you toward professions with particularly few opportunities for advancement. If, however, you believe that you will be financially well-off, you will expect to find opportunities that are consistent with this belief, and so these opportunities will arise.

Let's take inventory.

Find a blank piece of paper and draw a line down the middle. On the left side, list the beliefs you have about yourself and the world that give you strength. For example, "I believe I deserve to be happy and prosperous" is a positive belief. On the right side of the page list all the beliefs that weaken you. "I'll never lose this weight" would definitely be a negative belief and should be among those to be replaced with beliefs more consistent with your higher self.

Once you finish this exercise, you may be pleasantly surprised to see how many supportive beliefs you have about your potential, your future and all

"THERE IS NOT ANY PRESENT MOMENT THAT IS UNCONNECTED WITH SOME FUTURE ONE. THE LIFE OF EVERY MAN IS A CONTINUED CHAIN OF INCIDENTS, EACH LINK OF WHICH HANGS UPON THE FORMER."
—Joseph Addison, British poet

the wonderful personality traits that make you such an incredible person. If you list any negative beliefs about yourself (and most people do), write your answer to this question beside each one: "What do I need to do (what *action* do I need to take) to eliminate this negative belief?"

Most of the negative beliefs you have about yourself and the world will start to fade away once you see them in writing and realize how untrue they are.

In chapter seven, "Being Present," we discussed how Japa meditation can be used to create anything you want in life. You can also use Japa meditation to implant new positive beliefs in place of self-defeating ones. Again, see yourself, in your mind's eye, feeling and being in possession of the positive beliefs you want to plant in your life.

Before long you'll realize that who you are today and who you become tomorrow are both contingent on the dominant beliefs and expectations that you decide are true, real and believable. You and only you can decide what your beliefs will be. What beliefs do you need to have in order to get where you want to go? Here are a few suggestions:

I believe I am

sincere, kind, loving, funny, confident, fun, adventurous, romantic, grateful, sociable, ethical, honest, dependable, supportive, nurturing, successful, resourceful, nice, thoughtful, spontaneous, polite, creative, hard working, strong, forgiving, compassionate, generous, enthusiastic, worthy, optimistic, understanding, patient, tolerant, curious, fascinating, smart, prosperous, neighborly, modest, friendly, courageous, ambitious...

Which of these beliefs do you already have? Which ones do you need? Remember, believing is a verb. If you want to believe that you're a nice person—be a nice person!

EGO CONSCIOUSNESS

"HE ATTAINS PEACE WHO, GIVING UP DESIRE, MOVES THROUGH THE WORLD WITHOUT ASPIRATION, POSSESSING NOTHING WHICH HE CAN CALL HIS OWN, AND FREE FROM PRIDE."
—Bhagavad Gita

A Course in Miracles SAYS THAT "you have no problems, you only think you have." It does later concede, "You have one problem, your belief that you are separate from God." We live in a world where we have been conditioned to develop a consciousness that identifies who we are by how different and separate we are from everybody else, which is counterproductive to ever experiencing true happiness and a spiritual connection to the world.

The lower self experiences life through two types of consciousness: ego consciousness and group consciousness. Both of these negative realms of existence can prevent you from reaching the state of mind that we all desire. The goal of this chapter is to create an awareness that brings light to darkness, for the very core of each of these types of consciousness is filled with an energy that will weaken you if left unexposed. This negative energy is to your higher self what kryptonite is to Superman.

"THE EGO IS NOT MASTER IN ITS OWN HOUSE."
—Sigmund Freud, Austrian physician, founder of psychoanalysis

Our culture in the West promotes the illusion that the accumulation of *things* not only gives meaning to our lives, but is also a way of keeping score. The more things I have, the more successful I will appear to be and, so the theory goes, the happier I'll be. Any kind of peace of mind experienced through this shallow perspective will be short-lived, as we will forever be imprisoned in a world of comparing, competing and judging the "success" of other people. And just when we think we "have it all" we may notice our neighbor with the newer, sleeker, improved *thing*.

So we spend our existence working to be able to afford to buy the fancy car, the house in "the right neighborhood," the gold watch and whatever other things we believe we need in order to show the world that we measure up. Before too long, we've accumulated lots of things. The problem is, the old things we bought yesterday aren't as good as the new things we need today. Is it any wonder why, every spring in every city, there are garage sales on every street? We want to get rid of our stuff. The same stuff that made us feel great now makes us sick to see it—it's just junk now.

Your ego has a huge appetite and it is never satisfied for long. Do you remember how you felt when you bought your first big thing? Maybe it was a brand new car. Odds are you felt great. Odds are, as well, that you thought about what everyone was going to say when they saw you in your new car. For the first few weeks, life may have even been more exciting than it was before you bought the car. This type of "happiness for sale" experienced through

82

ego consciousness may last as long as the smell of the leather seats in your new car.

After a few months, not only is that new-car smell gone, so is the excitement. How does it happen? Let's say you are at home watching television and a commercial comes on advertising the same kind of car you just bought. Wow! Then they show the newer model. Your new car is now obsolete.

"Well, my next car is going to be even better," you tell yourself—and the cycle begins.

The constant barrage of advertising that we are subjected to on a daily basis teaches us to be envious of the people in the advertisements. You see, *they* have what *we* want. Or, at least, we are conditioned to believe that they have what we want. The intention of a successful advertisement campaign is to create the illusion that you will "measure up" after you buy a product, or worse, that you will remain incomplete without it.

A great example of how advertising manipulates our emotions to either buy (measure up) or not (remain incomplete) arises every year around Valentine's Day. A recent ad campaign by a diamond company featured a couple (presumably madly, deeply and passionately in love) on a romantic vacation. The couple is out walking when suddenly the man yells out for the whole world to hear: "I love this woman!" He then presents her with the rock. His lover takes one look at the diamond and says, "I love this man." The message? If you want her to say "I love you," you better go out and buy a diamond.

And that's not all! Other campaigns remind people who have been married for years that it's not

"CONCERN YOURSELF LESS WITH WHAT YOU HAVE THAN WITH WHAT YOU ARE, SO THAT YOU CAN BECOME AS EXCELLENT AS POSSIBLE."
—Socrates, Greek philosopher

"The bigger a man's head gets, the easier it is to feel his shoes."
—Anonymous

over yet—you still have to show your love by buying another diamond: "This year prove to her that you would marry her again with the diamond anniversary bracelet." It's no longer enough to spend three months' salary on the ring you propose with. More is always required. Love must always be proven with things.

It takes an enormous amount of energy to live in this realm of ego consciousness, not to mention the cost. Today, people have taken the question, "How much does happiness cost?" to levels no one could have predicted. Who would have thought that women would pay upwards of $10,000 to have a toxic substance injected into their bodies? And men would pay the same to have hair transplanted into their scalps?

Please don't misunderstand the message in this chapter. There is nothing wrong with wanting to have a beautiful appearance or nice things. However, looking to find happiness and connection to life by trying to fit into someone else's definition of who you should be, and substituting consumerism for spirituality will always keep the promise of fulfillment beyond your reach.

Real happiness, peace of mind and bliss can only be achieved through your connection to the world. Your connection to the world can be realized through practicing unity consciousness!

GROUP CONSCIOUSNESS

"WE CANNOT BE SEPARATED IN INTEREST OR DIVIDED IN PURPOSE. WE STAND TOGETHER UNTIL THE END."
—Woodrow T. Wilson, twenty-eighth President of the United States

*A*NOTHER SOURCE OF NEGATIVE energy is group consciousness. With group consciousness, you identify yourself with one group, thus allowing you to identify all other groups as separate from you. For example, you may say, "I'm Irish and you're English." Though it may go unsaid, there is often an underlying belief associated with this thought, something like "I'm Irish and my beliefs and values are better or more important than yours." This mindset can be applied to race, politics, gender and especially religion.

We all practice some form of group consciousness from time to time. Be honest with yourself and make a mental list of people, organizations, cultures and any other group that you see as "different" from yourself, even separate. Narrow it down to the groups that you feel anger, intolerance or even hate toward.

Of course, we witness and participate in group consciousness in seemingly harmless ways. As for me, I happen to ride a motorcycle. When I'm riding my motorcycle on the highway a very interesting thing happens: other motorcyclists wave to me as they ride by. They don't wave to the cars, trucks or pedestrians—just other motorcyclists. You see, I'm in the "club" where I'm being recognized by my fellow bikers; I'm recognized, valued and appreciated as "someone like me" to the other bikers.

Do you smoke cigars or know someone who smokes cigars? Cigars are promoted today as "one of the finer things in life," to be enjoyed by those who have "made it." They are, in many respects, what the members-only jackets symbolized years ago. We have been conditioned to crave this type of status. Why else would someone put a foreign object in his or her mouth which tastes like hot ash and may cause mouth, lip, throat and lung cancer, emphysema, high blood pressure and strokes? Do you think any four- or five-year-olds would want to smoke a big fat cigar?

Group consciousness, on its own, is not necessarily good or bad. But when we practice group consciousness to "one-up," or even de-humanize others whose values and beliefs are different from our own, it becomes possible, plausible and even thinkable to do the *unthinkable*.

As I write this book more than 6,500 people in Africa die every day of AIDS. Even though there is medicine available, we in the West let them die. In Rwanda, evidence continues to emerge that we stood by as more than 800,000 Tutsis and Hutu sympathizers were butchered in three months by the Hutu militia; U.N. forces were forbidden to intervene, as this would have breached their mandate, which was to "monitor" the situation only.

Today we stand by and do nothing as the Hema and Lendu kill each other in the Congo. If Rwanda or the Congo had the natural resources of Saudi Arabia or Iraq, do you think this would happen? If they presented a more direct threat to our lifestyle and peace of mind, would we let so many people die?

As long as we value things more than people and as long as we practice ego consciousness, there will continue to be an *us versus them* mentality in the world—a mentality that embodies a fear-based existence. If we stand by and do nothing as people around the world die of AIDS, starvation and genocide, as we worry about the cost of gas or whether the air-conditioning is working, we are as guilty of group consciousness as anyone.

And this phenomenon doesn't just exist from a global or national perspective. The FBI's Uniform Crime Reporting Program calculated that almost 7,500 hate crimes were reported to police in 2002. (You can imagine how many more occurred that went unreported.) Almost half the crimes were race-related, and thirty-three percent were against black people. Every day, somewhere in North America, a homeless person is attacked with a stun gun, racist graffiti is sprayed on someone's door, gravestones are knocked over and children are taunted ruthlessly by their peers. Why? Because of the insidious, blind ignorance that is born of group consciousness.

Religion is at the root of one of the most prevalent types of group consciousness. In many of the

"ALL FOR ONE, AND ONE FOR ALL."
—The Four Musketeers

87

so-called hot spots on the planet today—where bombs and bloodshed are daily events—some kind of religion-based group consciousness is at work. A deeply rooted hate has grown, for many complex reasons, out of a basic belief that "Our values are more important than yours, my God is more important than your God, and your beliefs are not as important as our beliefs. You are separate from us."

This kind of consciousness is not just simmering under the surface—it is very real. Speaking before the fifty-seven member nations of the Organization of the Islamic Conference, Malaysian prime minister Mahathir Mohamad called on the world's 1.3 billion Muslims to "defeat the Jews." He received a standing ovation for saying, "The Jews invented socialism, communism, human rights, and democracy so that persecuting them would appear to be wrong, so that they can enjoy equal rights with others." This speech wasn't given in 830 C.E. or 1400 C.E. This speech was given in 2003! It wasn't given by a convict, terrorist, murderer, or any other dangerous or insane person. The speech was given by a head of state who represents more than twenty-two million people. And he received a standing ovation from his peers.

We are often reminded, and reasonably so, that this kind of hatred is born out of many complicated economic, social and historical factors. But it is important to remember, also, that this hatred can exist in peaceful and peace-loving places like Canada. A small Muslim community newspaper in the town of Delta, British Columbia, published an article in December 2003, in which Jews were blamed for 9/11, both world wars and the Great Depression.

The question so many people in the West ask themselves is, "Where does so much hate come from?" The answer is not easy, especially if we are to avoid practicing group consciousness ourselves. There is, in a sense, a religious source for it, in the Quran. Quran 21:11 says, "And how many a town which was iniquitous did We demolish, and We raised up after it another people!" A theology degree is not required to see that statements like these could be manipulated by radical religious "leaders" to promote hate, intolerance and murder.

Mohammed (the founder of Islam) said, "The second most important duty of a follower is to wage *jihad* against the infidels." For the religious fanatic blinded by group consciousness, it is all too easy to manipulate these words to justify terror.

As we know, Christianity is no stranger to group consciousness. On November 27, 1095 C.E., Pope Urban II delivered a speech in France that would be remembered as the beginning of the first crusade. "The Franks must stop their internal wars and squabbles. Let them go instead against the infidel and fight a righteous war … It is God's will." And in God's will, thousands of Jews and Muslims were massacred. Examples like these can be found throughout history, within virtually any culture. Group consciousness is certainly not a modern phenomenon, nor does it belong to a certain group over another.

Of course God would never want us to kill one another. The kind of logic that promotes division

"A HOUSE DIVIDED AGAINST ITSELF CANNOT STAND—I BELIEVE THIS GOVERNMENT CANNOT ENDURE PERMANENTLY HALF SLAVE AND HALF FREE."
—Abraham Lincoln, sixteenth president of the United States

89

and hate can only be found in one place—the lower self.

Every war that has ever been fought and every act of genocide that has ever been committed has been in the name of group consciousness, no matter what the "official" story is.

I think we all know, deep down inside, that there is a God who goes by many (and sometimes multiple) names: God, Allah, Buddha, Brahman, Vishnu, and many others. As discussed way back at the beginning of this book, all the various religions in the world are *paths* to find God. It is humankind who divides and separates, not God. God is a mountain and there are literally an infinite number of paths to the top—one for everyone who lives and has ever lived. Remember the poem I quoted in the introduction? Let's look at it again together. These words are worth repeating:

Say not, "I have found the truth" but rather,
    "I have found a truth."
Say not, "I have found the path to the soul."
    Say rather, "I have met the soul walking
    upon my path."
For the soul walks on all paths.

There are great treasures of wisdom to be found in the Bible, the Quran, the Bhagavad Gita, the Torah and many other religious texts. When people ask me what religion I practice, my answer is always the same: "I practice all of them and none of them." I practice the truth, which can be found in all religions, but I refuse to say I belong to one or another when, in fact, there are no teams—just *paths*. And my path meanders through the wisdom of others—one day I'll read the Bible, the next I'll read the Bhagavad Gita and perhaps after that I'll read the Quran. Other days, I'll read great books with no religion directly attached to their message at all. They can all lead to peace and understanding.

Nearly two thousand years ago, Roman emperor Marcus Aurelius wrote:

> God sees the inner spirit stripped of flesh, skin, and all debris. For his own mind only touches the spirit that he has allowed to flow from himself into our bodies. And if you can act in the same way, you will rid yourself of all suffering.

Start to follow Marcus Aurelius' advice today. When you can look at another human being and see what God sees, you'll never feel alone or separate again! Nor will you have the need to practice any type of ego consciousness.

FEAR

"IT IS NOT DEATH THAT A MAN SHOULD FEAR, BUT HE SHOULD FEAR NEVER BEGINNING TO LIVE."
—Marcus Aurelius, Roman emperor, philosopher

*H*AVE YOU EVER NOTICED HOW OFTEN THE lead story on the evening news is about something or someone we should fear? Many large media empires today, motivated by ratings and market share, seem to be singing the same chorus: "If it bleeds, it leads."

I remember when news organizations simply reported the news. Walter Cronkite, the *CBS Evening News* anchor from 1962 to 1981, is known as one of the most trusted news personalities of all time. Not only was he valued for his accurate and unbiased reporting, but for how he closed the newscast by telling America, each and every night, "And that's the way it was. Goodnight." It was as though he was telling everyone that everything would be okay. Today, a more appropriate closing statement could be: "Goodnight. And God help us."

Today, the news is fast-paced and often graphic. Thanks to satellite technology, live breaking-news

"Do the thing you fear to do and keep on doing it ... that is the quickest and surest way ever yet discovered to conquer fear."
—Dale Carnegie, American author and trainer

updates can put the war in Iraq right in your living room. Today, people's fear is also fueled by the media in order to turn what should be a pretty average story into a News Event, complete with its own music and commercials. A few months ago, there was a storm on the south-eastern coast of the United States and Canada. It was a bad storm that meteorologists had given a rating of five, the highest possible. Of course, the news media took advantage. They sent in the troops within hours, even though the storm was several days away from even hitting the coastal states. It was almost amusing to watch the media spin the storm into "the mother of all storms" as they predicted the worst. But it was also frightening—even I worried about what would happen to the people whose homes would be flooded and lives threatened.

Since there were, as yet, no actual images of the storm to keep us tuned in, the media turned repeatedly to images of all the other storms of the past that created so much chaos and disaster. Experts from around the world were brought in to tell us what "could happen" if the storm went in this direction or that direction. The conclusion was always the same—complete chaos and destruction.

Meanwhile, the storm was downgraded to a category four, then three, then two. But the media seemed committed to keeping the fear alive. Even in the face of expert reports about the downgrading storm, journalists maintained their "positions" in the "front lines" of the storm (or what could have been a storm) until the very end. It wasn't until days later that I realized that my fear, and everyone else's, was created to keep me hooked to every news break.

We see this type of sensationalism repeated on a daily basis. "Tune in tonight to learn more about the new threat against homeland security, the new flu virus, computer virus (remember Y2K?), West Nile virus . . . and if that's not enough, how about violence?"

"Violent crime has gone down by twenty percent in the last ten years, yet the media's coverage of violent crime has increased by more than 600 percent," according to sociology professor Barry Glassner in *The Culture of Fear*, published in 1999. Is it any wonder we're so fearful? Often the media will show footage of a violent or disturbing image over and over and over again, as they speculate why it happened, how it happened, if it is going to happen again and who could get hurt. All this despite, as Henry David Thoreau said, "someone dying in an accident ceases to be news after you've heard it once."

Even the food we eat cannot escape the media's doom-and-gloom perspective. One week, there's a news item about a miracle vegetable that decreases the risk of developing certain types of cancers only to be followed up the next week with breaking news that the same vegetable also increases the risk of developing some other cancers. Of course, journalists among you will say: "The people deserve to know." And they do. But remember the earlier discussion about the words we use and their power over our mood. Fear-mongering as a way to make a living is just the kind of negative energy that eats away at the higher self.

"FOR IT IS NOT DEATH OR HARDSHIP THAT IS A FEARFUL THING, BUT THE FEAR OF DEATH AND HARDSHIP."
—Epictetus, Stoic philosopher

"YOU GAIN
STRENGTH,
COURAGE, AND
CONFIDENCE BY
EACH EXPERIENCE
IN WHICH YOU
REALLY STOP TO
LOOK FEAR IN THE
FACE. YOU ARE
ABLE TO SAY TO
YOURSELF, 'I HAVE
LIVED THROUGH
THIS HORROR. I
CAN TAKE THE
NEXT THING THAT
COMES ALONG.'
YOU MUST DO THE
THING YOU THINK
YOU CANNOT DO."
—Eleanor
Roosevelt,
American First
Lady

And remember the other saying journalists have: "A picture is worth a thousand words." Even our most popular television entertainment programs are feeding us fear. According to a 1998 study by the American Psychological Association, children are exposed to 8,000 murders and 100,000 acts of violence on TV by the time they finish elementary school.

When three of the most-watched television shows in North America today are aired in Canada there's a warning after every commercial: "This program contains scenes of graphic violence which may be upsetting to some viewers." And there is some evidence that this warning actually boosts viewership among teenagers! It's like we've become oblivious to what our soul is being fed day in and day out. We've become like the guy who ate greasy burgers everyday for twenty years, had a heart attack and wondered how it happened.

We've been conditioned to believe, "it's okay, it's just entertainment … it's not like its real or anything." But your subconscious mind does not know the difference between fantasy and reality—it doesn't have a filter that tells it to dismiss what it's seeing as fantasy (which is why nightmares are so scary). When you watch murder after murder, cheating, lying, corruption and misery, know that this type of spiritual diet is damaging to your soul. All this "entertainment" is taking you further and further away from the kind of bliss that your higher self is craving to experience.

Yes, we do live in a fear-based society. But where do these often harmful thoughts come from? Look back, for a moment, at when you were a kid. Often, growing up, we'd hear comments like, "Don't go out after dark," or "Don't talk to strangers," or later, "Don't work on commission." We've been taught to seek guarantees and, in turn, to avoid any type of situation with an unknown factor in it. Our parents wanted us to be safe, of course, but what were they doing to our spiritual life when they convinced us that the unknown was, by definition, dangerous?

If you're at a wedding, in the receiving line, and as you approach the bride and groom you say, "I sure hope it works out," there's a good chance you won't be invited to any more weddings! But, in life, that's exactly what we do; we hope things turn out a certain way and in the process spend much of our time fearing what might happen.

This type of behavior is similar to what a deer does when a car approaches it on the road. The deer is "caught" in the headlights, as though they have some kind of magnetic pull. Like those headlights, fear immobilizes us. It teaches us to avoid taking many of the kinds of risks necessary for growth, whether in business, in relationships or in our own personal transformation.

But honestly, what is happening two Tuesdays from this time next year? What is the weather going to be like in three weeks? Who is your neighbor going to be in three years? What we all need is a perspective shift.

Perspective Shift

Okay, let's say you are walking down the street and you meet a friend. After some pleasantries are

"THOSE WHO FEAR THE FUTURE ARE LIKELY TO FUMBLE THE PRESENT."
—Anonymous

"WE ARE MORE
OFTEN FRIGHT-
ENED THAN HURT;
AND WE SUFFER
MORE FROM IMAGI-
NATION THAN
FROM REALITY."
-Seneca, Spanish-
born Roman
philosopher

exchanged, you ask, "Hey, have you seen any great movies lately?" Your friend says, "Oh ya, I just saw that new James Bond movie," and then proceeds to tell you about the movie in full detail—I mean frame by frame. Well, I think that in this case we can all agree to politely ask this friend not to tell us the entire movie because we might want to see it ourselves. Why? Because not knowing is part of the enjoyment that comes with seeing a movie. We actually look forward to the "not knowing."

The anticipation of letting the movie happen before our eyes is what going to a movie is all about. We are curious to see how things are going to work out. As we sit, eating our popcorn, we say to ourselves, "I wonder what's going to happen next." We certainly don't fear what's going to happen next—except maybe in that delicious, thrilling way that keeps people riveted.

If we did know what was going to happen—if we sought a guaranteed ending—wouldn't that be boring? And so it is with life when we continue to look for guarantees.

Perhaps we can look at our life as a movie—one that doesn't end and has breaks while we sleep to set up the new adventures for the next day. Imagine living a life where you are the producer, director and have the leading role in a movie called *This Is My Life*. Try this perspective shift and you may be more willing to let life happen—to spend your time in the moment, thinking about the moment instead of worrying about a future that hasn't happened yet. You get to write your next scene. Imagine living a life that welcomes uncertainty instead of fearing it.

Continuing on the movie theme, let's look at some of our favorite heroes for a minute. Would you really want to see Indiana Jones contemplate all the things that could happen, sitting in his office worrying about all the ways he could get hurt if he pursued the priceless relic? "Face your fears," you would tell him. "Show me some action!" If he didn't get his act together, you would walk out of the theater. How thrilled would you be to dish out twenty bucks (when you add popcorn and a drink—gotta have that!) to watch a Spiderman who is afraid of heights? No, we love seeing these movies because we know that all these action heroes have one thing in common—they don't live in fear; they welcome any challenge and they expect to win!

Don't worry about all the uncertainties of tomorrow—how you're going to pay the bills, whether or not you're going to get the big contract or what the weather is going to be like. You can't control these things. The only thing you can control is your response. Welcome the uncertainty of tomorrow with a healthy sense of curiosity.

So, tomorrow when you awaken to star in the continuation of the hit movie *This Is My Life,* be the hero that you know you're capable of being and give the Oscar-winning performance that you know you were made to give!

ACTION!

"THE GREATEST MISTAKE YOU CAN MAKE IN THIS LIFE IS TO BE CONSTANTLY FEARFUL YOU WILL MAKE ONE."
—Anonymous

"THERE ARE ONLY
TWO DAYS A WEEK
THAT I DON'T
WORRY ABOUT:
YESTERDAY AND
TOMORROW."
—Derrick Sweet

WORRY IS

ORRYING—A CLOSE FRIEND OF FEAR—is also hazardous to your peace of mind. We all worry from time to time about the events that are happening in our life, the people we love and the challenges of the day. Worrying to the point of getting stressed out, developing ulcers, high blood pressure or heart disease, however, can take much of the joy out of life and even lead to an early grave.

Again, worry comes from fear about what may happen in the future. This fear of what may happen, or not happen, in the future can paralyze you like that deer in headlights, keeping you in a constant state of panic.

Fear comes in all shapes and colors, and its buddy worry does too. Fear of criticism may cause you to constantly worry about what other people think and say about you. Fear of poverty may cause you to worry about losing your job. Fear of loneliness may cause you to worry about your marriage

101

"THERE IS NOTH-
ING THAT WASTES
THE BODY LIKE
WORRY, AND ONE
WHO HAS ANY
FAITH IN GOD
SHOULD BE
ASHAMED TO
WORRY ABOUT
ANYTHING WHAT-
SOEVER."
—Mahatma
Ghandi, political
and spiritual leader

ending in divorce. It can be so bad that you begin to *expect* the marriage to end. Fear of flying may cause you to worry about the plane crashing as you begin your journey and allow a shadow of uneasiness to be cast over your entire trip. Did you know that you are ten times more likely to perish in the bathtub than you are in a plane crash?

Again, worry is created by fear, and fear is based on your determination to seek guarantees. Napoleon Hill, author of *Think And Grow Rich*, said, "Nothing which life has to offer is worth the price of worry." The day you decide that the price of worrying is too high will be the day you start to loosen worry's grip on your life.

The first step to overcoming worry is to stop scouring the fine print for guarantees. Your marriage might not work out, your company could get downsized and your favorite television program could even get cancelled. I've said it before and I'll say it again: the only thing that you can control in life is your reaction to what is happening to you.

You will be free of all fear when you decide to stop worrying about all the hypothetical what-if scenarios that may or may not happen in the future. You will be free of all worry when you decide to spend your energy on what you do control. What you do control is your ability to *choose* how you will think, how you will react and how you will feel about everything that is happening in your life.

You can vanquish worry from your life forever when you realize that all you have to do is *choose* to stop worrying. You can choose to live or you can choose to worry! It's really up to you.

Of course, bad things are going to happen to you. They do, to everyone. But when they do, you will have practiced making choices about how you react. You will have built up strength in your higher self to support you through it. You will have gained insight into yourself and your world so that negative events—as big as a parent's death and as small as a traffic jam—will not cause you to crumble.

After all, worry isn't going to stop these bad things from happening, is it? Worry can't control the weather, other people or the economy. All it does is rob you of the present, when things are good. So drop the worry! Face the moment.

"THE REASON WHY WORRY KILLS MORE PEOPLE THAN WORK IS BECAUSE MORE PEOPLE WORRY THAN WORK."
—Robert Frost, American poet

(16) NEGATIVE BELIEFS

"QUIT THINKING THAT YOU MUST HALT BEFORE THE BARRIER OF INNER NEGATIVITY. YOU NEED NOT. YOU CAN CRASH THROUGH WHEREVER WE SEE A NEGATIVE STATE, THAT IS WHERE WE CAN DESTROY IT."
—Vernon Howard, American author

*E*ARLIER, I COMPARED YOUR CONSCIOUSNESS to a garden. This garden will grow whatever seeds are planted. Unfortunately, most people are going through life letting the news media, advertising, family members, coworkers and others' agendas determine what seeds are planted in their garden.

Every morning, as you listen to the latest news, notice how the violence committed in our cities mirrors the violent programming fed to our youth in the television they watch, the music they listen to and the video games they play. Is it really just entertainment? Or is something else happening? Do we not become what we feel and perceive? The very real anger and fear you experience while watching a violent television program spreads like a virus throughout the entirety of our soul; we become angry and fearful. And what about our humor? What makes us laugh, these days? Let's take a look at what's on late-night television.

105

"THERE IS LITTLE
DIFFERENCE IN
PEOPLE, BUT THAT
LITTLE DIFFERENCE
MAKES A BIG
DIFFERENCE. THAT
LITTLE DIFFERENCE
IS ATTITUDE. THE
BIG DIFFERENCE IS
WHETHER IT IS
POSITIVE OR
NEGATIVE."
—W. Clement
Stone, American
businessman

Listen (with mindfulness) to hosts' opening monologues each evening as they exploit the latest misfortunes of the celebrities of the day. I recently paid a visit to the *Late Show with David Letterman* website to listen to a monologue from the previous night. It takes no time for the negativity to begin. "How about that Michael Jackson?" Mr. Letterman says. "They finally came up with a mug shot that's scarier than Nick Nolte's." The crowd laughs. "We're right in the middle of cold and flu season. It's gotten so bad here in New York City ... I'm in my cab and my taxi driver was blowing his nose in his turban."

If Letterman worked for a Fortune 500 company and said these hateful remarks in public he would be fired immediately. But the crowd laughs, not being fully present to what is happening. You can argue that what he said was funny, that his job is to make people laugh, and he is doing that. But that's not the point. Think instead about what hosts like Letterman are promoting. This kind of humor, which is heard in barber shops across the country, at work and at home is prejudice—plain and simple. And putting it in the mainstream legitimizes it. I mean, Letterman is considered mild compared to a lot of what's aired today. Is it any wonder why so many people practice group consciousness?

After I listened to Letterman for a few minutes, I thought I'd check out his competition. I tuned in to *The Tonight Show* website and heard Jay Leno say, "Here you go ... more gossip. There are rumors that Prince Charles may have had a homosexual affair. Turns out a witness to the incident just mistook Camilla Parker Bowles for a guy."

On the surface, these comments may seem innocent enough, maybe even funny. You may think, "Hey, they're just teasing and don't mean any harm." I don't think Jay Leno or David Letterman are mean people. However, this brand of humor, if you can call it that, is teaching us to be insensitive toward others, especially to their misfortunes. As kids we were told, "Don't point," "Don't stare" and "Don't laugh when someone is hurt." But as adults, it is acceptable to mock people in the name of humor. Is it any wonder we fear how the public (our friends, co-workers, even family) would react if we took the proverbial slip on the banana peel?

A close relative to this kind of humor is gossip. Office talk is so commonly laced with gossip that many don't even notice it anymore. Today, there is a thriving industry focused on creating, promoting and selling gossip. It should come as no surprise that one of the most popular magazines in America today is the *National Enquirer*, which is chock full of innuendoes, rumors and mean-spiritedness. Why do we torture ourselves this way?

Another unlimited stream of negativity can be found on C-SPAN, a public service channel provided by cable and satellite companies that shows politics in action. I'm not sure which is worse, Chinese water torture or watching C-SPAN for more than five minutes. Any time there is a debate between two or more political parties, the name-calling, judging, accusations and downright nastiness begins. It is amazing to think that the so-called decision makers of a country sound basically like so many squabbling children!

"WE HAVE BEEN TAUGHT TO BELIEVE THAT NEGATIVE EQUALS REALISTIC AND POSITIVE EQUALS UNREALISTIC."
—Susan Jeffers, American author, lecturer

"People deal too much with the negative, with what is wrong. Why not try and see positive things, to just touch those things and make them bloom?"
—Thich Nhat Hanh, Buddhist monk

Exercise

Make a list of any negative content that you allow into your consciousness. This list could include certain television programs, books, tabloids or gossip with co-workers and friends. It may also include your ongoing self-talk—the longest conversation you'll ever have.

Next, list the long-term impact of each negative activity or habit. And finally, list what kinds of positive activities you can create to replace the negative ones.

If you're oblivious to your every thought, you end up wherever you end up, and it is usually not where you ultimately want to go. When you play a conscious role in the unfolding of your life, you may suddenly realize how powerful an effect every single (even seemingly insignificant) decision, habit, thought and action has on the quality of life you experience.

"HE CANNOT BE
STRICT IN JUDGING,
WHO DOES NOT
WISH OTHERS TO
BE STRICT JUDGES
OF HIMSELF."
—Marcus T.
Cicero, Roman
politician

JUDGING & CRITICIZING

*A*LL WE WANT, AT OUR ESSENCE, IS to be accepted. And perhaps our greatest longing is self-acceptance. But as long as we continue to judge others, self-acceptance will remain an impossibility.

When we judge others, we often do so with the self-righteous, vindictive spirit of the lower self. The lower self is motivated by fear, jealousy and ignorance. It constantly finds faults in the character of others as a means of self-preservation.

We only judge others when our lower self feels threatened. This is more likely to happen when the actions and beliefs of others are in conflict with our own perception of how we think the world should work. (Please read chapter eighteen, "Attachment," for more information.)

Often, we don't even realize when we're judging others. Have you ever caught yourself waiting in line at the grocery store, scanning other people's goodies as you wait for your turn to pay? You may

"ANY FOOL CAN CRITICIZE, CONDEMN AND COMPLAIN AND MOST FOOLS DO."
—Benjamin Franklin, American politician

have commented to yourself, "Why is that lady with all the sweets, pastries and microwavable meals buying diet cola? What's the point lady? You may as well just buy the real thing [no pun intended] cause you ain't on no diet."

On the highway, on your way to work, have you ever caught yourself judging the driving skills of your fellow commuters? Have you ever uttered comments like, "Where the @!*# did you learn to drive, you idiot!?!" In restaurants, have you judged your server for service that wasn't quite up to your expectations? Still haven't stumped you? Okay, what about your in-laws?

Our habit of judging is a by-product of being angry and disconnected. Think about it: do you judge others when you're in complete harmony with the world? Ram Dass, one of the most enlightened spiritual teachers of recent years says, "When you look at anger, you will find judgment. Give up judgment, and then you will have clear compassion."

If you weren't so fearful of being judged yourself, would you be so hard on people? Would you be such a critic if you weren't so worried about being criticized yourself? Do you think God sits up there on the "Holy Throne" judging and criticizing? God knows that only hell can be found in such negative quests.

Next time you judge or criticize or listen to someone else judge or criticize, allow yourself to be mindful of how heavy the mood becomes. Know this: every single time you judge or criticize others, you are moving further away from what you want to create in your life. It takes incredible discipline to be mindful of every single time you judge others.

However, when you become mindful of the damage you do to yourself by judging and criticizing others, you may become quite motivated to quit this self-defeating habit.

I'm about to give you a formula to help you stop judging others forever. Before I give you this formula I should warn you of two things you should know:

It sounds too easy (I know it does—but it works).

It is really silly (Yes, it is silly).

Now that we've got this little acknowledgement out of the way, we can move on to the exercise. As I said at the beginning of this book, people seem to be looking for complicated solutions to their problems in life; perhaps a formula with some trigonometry or calculus in it would be more believable. Sorry, this is more like learning your ABCs.

Okay, here it is. The next time you catch yourself judging or criticizing someone, do the following:

1) Notice how it makes you feel. Allow yourself to feel the sheer weight of the negativity. Then say, to yourself, "YUCK!" You can say it out loud, as well, but you may receive some odd looks.

2) Immediately after you say, "YUCK!" think of a sincere compliment (you have to mean it!) that you could say in the place of the judgment. Now notice how much better you feel.

Sounds like an easy enough exercise, right? Wrong! Remember, you do have a lower self who wants no part in this "stupid exercise." You may also have some pride, which can get in the way. Pride

"WHATEVER YOU DO, YOU NEED COURAGE. WHATEVER COURSE YOU DECIDE UPON, THERE IS ALWAYS SOMEONE TO TELL YOU THAT YOU ARE WRONG. THERE ARE ALWAYS DIFFICULTIES ARISING THAT TEMPT YOU TO BELIEVE YOUR CRITICS ARE RIGHT. TO MAP OUT A COURSE OF ACTION AND FOLLOW IT TO AN END REQUIRES SOME OF THE SAME COURAGE THAT A SOLDIER NEEDS. PEACE HAS ITS VICTORIES, BUT IT TAKES BRAVE MEN AND WOMEN TO WIN THEM."
—Ralph Waldo Emerson, American author

111

"CRITICS ARE
THOSE WHO HAVE
FAILED IN LITERA-
TURE AND ART."
—Benjamin
Disraeli, British
prime minister

wants nothing to do with this exercise because there's no trigonometry in it.

Your ego—and yes, we all have one—wants you to believe that you are separate from everybody and everything (see chapter twelve, "Ego Consciousness"), and uses judgment as a means to keep this illusion alive. Even if you try this exercise just once, your ego will be eclipsed by your immediate sense of unity, interconnectedness and bliss. These are all the warm, wonderful by-products of empathy. No judgment can survive in its presence.

(18) ATTACHMENT

"WHEN YOU MOVE AMIDST THE WORLD OF SENSE, FREE FROM ATTACHMENT AND AVERSION ALIKE, THERE COMES THE PEACE IN WHICH ALL SORROWS END, AND YOU LIVE IN THE WISDOM OF THE SELF."
—Bhagavad Gita

MORE THAN 2,500 YEARS AGO, the great Buddha said, "Attachment leads to suffering." When I first read these words I was confused. What's wrong with being attached to things, people and one's expectations of life?

I now realize that the problem is that being attached prevents you from truly living in the moment. The joy, ecstasy and awe that can be experienced in the moment is often overpowered by the fear of loss that accompanies attachment.

When we abandon our attachment to things, people and expectations, we soon notice a feeling of liberation. A feeling of calm replaces the anxiety, stress and worry of attachment. Of course, abandoning attachment to people doesn't mean you care for your loved ones any less. It just means you become free of the lower energies like fear of loss, jealousy and resentment that often accompany attachment in relationships.

For the first three years of my marriage to Marsha, I was attached to the idea of being married to Marsha. That seems pretty normal, right? Maybe it is, but is it healthy for the relationship? Because I was so attached to the need for certainty—for a guarantee somewhere in the fine print—that we would stay together forever, I wasted many of my precious moments worrying about the future. What if she meets another man? What if we drift apart? What if we fall out of love? It's enough to drive you crazy. And that's exactly what happens to many people who live in the world of attachment.

Once I abandoned my attachment to Marsha, our relationship began to evolve. Rather than focusing on being together forever, I became focused on this moment. With the heavy baggage of attachment gone, I had room to just be with Marsha rather than with my worries about the future. It certainly was a good trade!

Now wait a minute, you may say, what about all my action plans, my manifesting of the future? In a previous chapter, we discussed the benefits of having expectations that support the vision of your higher self. And these are important. But having expectations is not the same as being attached to those expectations. When we are rigidly attached to certain expectations, we are blinded to all the opportunities that present themselves during the course of our day-to-day activities.

Let's say you're going out to your favorite restaurant for your favorite dish, Chicken Florentine. All day you've been anticipating the smell, taste and satisfaction of experiencing your favorite meal. Yum!

You arrive, sit at your favorite table and place your order. You can almost taste it now! You wait, savoring the anticipation of enjoying your favorite meal, knowing that your appetite is about to be satisfied. After five minutes, the waiter informs you that the restaurant is out of chicken. Now, if you are attached to Chicken Florentine and nothing else, you will likely react in a negative manner, ruining your mood, not to mention that of the friend you're with, the waiter and maybe even the people at the next table. "What kind of restaurant is this?" you may say, your voice rising. Your mood changes from happiness to disappointment and frustration.

Practicing attachment creates a feeling of having no control in your life, making you a victim of circumstance. Of course, you can't control situations like the Chicken Florentine fiasco. You can only control one thing—your response. The best way to control your response is to preempt it completely by shedding your attachment to specific scenarios and allowing yourself to be open to opportunities.

When you allow yourself to be detached from certainty, suddenly an awakening of awareness occurs that gives you the ability to see what attachment could not. Suddenly you develop an appetite for the spaghetti or the clams or the green salad with endive. When you shed your attachment, you stop seeking guarantees, you stop feeling disappointed or victimized. You suddenly notice a wonderful shift in the way you see, feel and experience life!

For most of us, we identify our "self" as a body and a mind, together. When our bodies catch a cold, we say, "I'm sick," not "My body is sick."

"HE WHO BINDS TO HIMSELF A JOY DOES THE WINGED LIFE DESTROY; BUT HE WHO KISSES THE JOY AS IT FLIES LIVES IN ETERNITY'S SUNRISE."
—William Blake, English poet

115

When our minds feel confused or frustrated, we say, "I am frustrated!" We don't say, "My mind is experiencing frustration."

But where is your higher self in this picture? Remember, it is completely detached from the body's moods, problems and the entire goings-on of the physical self. The higher self is not a part of your physical life; it is the *witness* to your physical life. And, your goal is to see life through the eyes of the witness. Your perspective on everything changes in the instant you are able to do that.

Earlier in this book, I quoted Ralph Waldo Emerson. Now, take a look at the rest of the quotation, where we can consider "him" to refer to the body and mind, and "the soul" to be the higher self:

> Him we do not respect, but the soul, whose organ he is, would he let it appear through his action, would make our knees bend. When it breathes through his intellect, it is genius; when it breathes through his will, it is virtue; when it flows through his affection, it is love.
> —Ralph Waldo Emerson (1803–1882), *Essays and English Traits*

As many of the examples so far have shown (traffic jams, missing the Chicken Florentine, judging others), so much of our misery comes from taking what's happening in our life so personally. This is the major purpose of the lower self: to create a world where control is sought and lost, where change means failure and where harmony between people is an illusion—it's been ingrained in our consciousness since birth. Be the witness and you will rise above this lower self consciousness. As Emerson said, your body and mind will experience genius, virtue and love. What else is that but heaven on earth?

Of course, fear will continue to pay you a visit from time to time. But be the witness and you won't make the same mistakes of the lower self, which internalizes negative emotions, physical ailments and fear. Let's say that you aren't the most outgoing person in the world and your boss informs you that in one week you are to give a report to your fellow employees on the progress you've been making on a certain project.

When we experience life through our lower self, we use our imagination in ways that take us further away from the results we are hoping to achieve. We imagine the worst: forgetting part of our speech, looking stupid in front of our peers and even getting fired for looking like such an idiot. All these images are quite normal when we internalize (through attachment) our emotions, as the lower self has taught us to do.

Next time any negative emotion invades your mind, allow yourself to become the witness. Instead of saying, "I'm so stressed out right now," you'll be more inclined to say, "My body is really stressed out right now." Go ahead and say the two responses; you'll notice how helpless the lower self response is, whereas the witness is always calm, cool and collected.

Seeking congruency, the lower self will only seek more proof to support the claim that you are

"WHEN YOU BEGIN YOUR TRANSCENDENTAL TRAINING, FOCUSING YOUR BEST EFFORTS, WITHOUT ATTACHMENT TO OUTCOMES, YOU WILL UNDERSTAND THE PEACEFUL WARRIOR'S WAY."
—Dan Millman, American author

stressed out. "Of course you're stressed out, what's-his-name never does anything! I do everything around here," barks the lower self. The higher self, standing witness, will be more likely to give a loving response that is focused on supporting your long-term objectives: "This stress my body is feeling is okay, but it's not going to make me forget what's important; I work hard and I will do the best I can."

By recognizing that you are experiencing stress at this moment, the higher self allows you to find a remedy for the situation. The witness has no desire to fan the flames of negativity; it knows that this event has not occurred "just to make you crazy." It doesn't take it personally. The witness is more likely to respond with a comment like, "Your body is stressed, which isn't helping you solve your problem, so how about a nice hot bath?" This subtle shift in consciousness will prevent you from internalizing (becoming attached) to the events that happen in your life.

As you sit in the bubbles, you will begin to plan out your speech. You will visualize how you want it to go—you may even see your boss calling you into her office to offer you that promotion. Think of the confidence you'll feel as you walk into your meeting the next day! With the negative emotions that accompany attachment removed, your actions and emotions will naturally start to be consistent with the intentions of your higher self.

VISUALIZATION

*I*N 1950, ADVERTISING EXPERT JAMES VICARY began testing subliminal advertising in movie theaters across the United States. He inserted the words, "eat popcorn" and "drink cola" into the frames of the film, but just for a split-second—not long enough so that the audience could consciously read them. Despite not seeing the words, the audience's purchases of cola increased by eighteen percent and popcorn by an unbelievable fifty-eight percent!

This experiment confirmed what the great philosophers have been saying for thousands of years: the subconscious mind creates your reality by influencing your thoughts, feelings and actions. Whatever you consciously or unconsciously think about (like eating popcorn) gets programmed in your subconscious mind. These cumulative images, feelings and thoughts influence how you react to the ongoing events of your life.

In other words, your thoughts, programmed into

your subconscious mind, are eventually used to create an environment that is congruent with this programming. Understanding this self-mastery principle will allow you to develop your higher self to whatever level you wish to achieve. If you are shy and wish to become more outgoing or assertive, simply visualizing yourself being more outgoing or assertive will influence your behavior in the future.

Remember, I said earlier, in my discussion on violence, that your subconscious mind does not register the difference between fantasy and reality. You can use this to your advantage. When you visualize yourself acting, feeling or behaving in a manner that is consistent with your true aspirations, this pattern of memories, feelings and emotions is just as real to your subconscious mind as the "real thing" would be. Of course, the real benefit of visualizing is that because your subconscious mind seeks congruent experiences, it becomes possible to perform, in reality, the specific act that you visualized yourself doing. In this way, your true aspirations become attainable.

You may have heard the story of Major James Nesmeth, an American prisoner of war in North Vietnam. For the seven years he was held in solitary confinement in a cage that was approximately four-and-a-half feet high and five feet long, Major Nesmeth was not allowed any physical activity.

Major Nesmeth quickly realized that he had to find some way to take his mind off the terrible conditions. He chose to imagine playing golf. Every day, he imagined (visualized) playing a perfect game of golf at his favorite golf course. He never missed a shot. When he was finally released and had the opportunity to play a real game of golf, he took twenty strokes off his best game, to shoot a seventy-four.

If this exercise sounds too good to be true, too simple to work, I want you to realize that you have already been practicing this exercise your whole life. Think about it.

Do you remember a time when you had to do something that you were fearful of? Maybe you had to give a speech in school and were terrified or had to go to a ceremony of some kind that you didn't want to attend. By thinking of all the bad things that could have gone wrong or reasons why things wouldn't work out, your subconscious mind was programmed to expect a negative experience. Now that you know this, it is possible to challenge this negative programming with something better.

HOW TO USE AFFIRMATIONS
TO CREATE HEAVEN ON EARTH

FFIRMATIONS ARE DECLARATIONS you make to the universe about what you want to create for yourself. When making affirmations, your conscious thoughts act like a software program that you download to your subconscious mind—your hard drive. Your hard drive determines how you think, feel and act, thereby creating your reality.

In a previous chapter, we discussed the power of Japa meditation to manifest what you desire in life. Repeating affirmations at the conclusion or beginning of your meditation will produce powerful results, if practiced regularly and with faith and emotion. You must be able to see, feel and fully experience the event in your mind, as if it were really happening. This is a great exercise to discover how powerful your imagination really is.

The following affirmations are merely suggestions you may use in your meditations. My advice is to use the ones that resonate with you and leave the rest. If you can, write a few of your own affirmations for each of the important areas of your life. For example, you may include your career, your relationships, your health, your state of mind or your spiritual connection to the world.

If you do write a few more personal affirmations, structure them as if they are already true. This will create a more realistic impression on your subconscious. You don't necessarily have to meditate to use these affirmations. You can take a copy of them with you on a quiet walk in the woods. Find a nice spot to sit down and then simply read each affirmation, one at a time, allowing yourself to actually feel the power of each phrase.

Affirmations

Today I release any self-imposed limitations, negative thoughts and disempowering beliefs.

Today I embrace my higher self.

Today I breathe in the positive energies of the universe and I breathe out all self-imposed limitations. *[Actually allow yourself to feel the energy with each breath!]*

Today I do not judge others but rather practice tolerance and acceptance.

Today I see God in all living creatures, even the ones disguised as separate from me.

Today I attract people, opportunities and situations into my life that support the desires of my higher self.

Today I embrace each moment with the excitement, joy and love that I would offer a long-lost friend.

Today I am present in this moment and give this moment a hundred percent of my very best!

Today I am not holding back in any way. I am doing what needs to be done, I am saying what needs to be said and I am loving who needs to be loved.

Today I am grateful for all the abundance in my life.

Today I find all the answers I need in the universal consciousness through Japa.

Today I am aware of all the beauty, opportunities and bliss that surround me.

I realize that my dominating beliefs create my life, therefore I only choose positive beliefs.

Today I fear nothing and know that the only thing to fear is fear itself.

Today I choose to tame, make peace with and silence my lower self.

Today I am living my life on purpose, which gives my life meaning. *[Think of your purpose.]*

My purpose serves a worthy cause. *[Think of your purpose.]*

(21) FINAL THOUGHTS

*T*HIS BOOK WAS WRITTEN TO BE A COM-
panion to my other book, *Get the Most
Out of Life*. I would like to close now
with what may be considered a bold comment. I
really believe that if you keep copies of *Get the Most
Out of Life* and *You Don't Have to Die to Go to
Heaven* somewhere nearby—in the bathroom, on
the coffee table or in your briefcase or purse—you'll
become a happier person. I'd like you to think of
both these books as reminders of what you already
know intuitively. Like wise old friends, they will
always be there to keep you on track and remind
you to do what you should be doing.

Because we still live in a world that caters to the
belief that we are all separate, a world that broad-
casts, "You better get your piece of the action before
the competition," life can seem a little meaningless
at times. Well, those times are the perfect times to
pick up one of these books, to remind yourself that
all this lower self stuff is just an illusion; the only

thing that is real, here on 123 Main Street, Everywhere, Earth 92281, is your connection to me and my connection to you and our connection to divinity. There is nothing more important than this simple truth, nor is there anything more powerful!

If you only remember this final thought you'll know, indeed, that you don't have to die to go to heaven.

Thank you for giving me this privilege to share my thoughts with you. I would love to hear your feedback. If any thought or exercise has made a difference in your life, I would love to know about it. Please contact me at:

dsweet@healthywealthyandwise.com

or send your thoughts to:

The Healthy Wealthy and Wise Corporation
1 Yonge Street, Suite 1801
Toronto, Ontario, Canada
M5E 1W7

All the best,

Derrick Sweet

GLOSSARY

Action plan

This book often describes how to change your thinking, attitude or perspective on yourself and the world. It shows you the importance of your self-talk, of generosity and of living on purpose. For many of us, this change will not happen all by itself. An action plan is any kind of structured proposal for achieving change. The key word here is *action*: you must create a step-by-step guide to achieve change within yourself. This could involve meditation, reading or changing what you eat or how you communicate with others. The point is, it's always one step at a time. And when you have a plan, you know where to begin.

Attachment

That attachment is negative can be confusing to many people, at first glance. It seems only natural to become attached to the things, people and experiences that we want in our lives. But the trouble is, attachment leads to too many negative emotions like jealousy, fear and guilt. It also closes you off from the opportunities that you are exposed to each and every day. Being free of attachment means being free of fear and loss. Imagine, for a moment, what such freedom would feel like.

Buddhism

Buddhism was founded in 525 B.C.E. by Siddhartha Gautama (Buddha). The basic idea behind it is that all suffering in life comes from craving and attachment. The "eightfold path" to the cessation of suffering involves right views, right resolve, right speech, right action, right livelihood, right effort, right mindfulness and right concentration.

Collective consciousness

This powerful idea, described at length by David Hawkins in *Power vs. Force*, can be traced back to Carl Jung, whose idea of an individual's mind being connected to a universal subconscious has influenced countless thinkers after him. The idea is that there exists a distilled essence of humanity that contains all the collected thoughts of every person who ever lived.

Ego consciousness

Essentially, this type of thinking is the opposite of unity consciousness. It is what makes you compare yourself to others (negatively or positively). It is also what makes you seek out things (like a new car) and thrills (like sky-diving or an affair). As you might guess, it breeds the unhappiness that comes from a sense that something is missing in your life.

Group consciousness

This type of consciousness, a product of your lower self, tells you that, in big and small ways, you are separate from your fellow human beings, and by extension, separate from God. It is what lies behind every hate crime, terrorist act and snub at the office party. It is driven by fear of the unknown, and it prevents compassion and true bliss.

Higher self

The higher self is the part of you that has the power to act as a witness to your everyday experience. It is the part of you that experiences your connection to the universe, and it is the part of you that allows you to realize heaven on earth. It is sometimes called the soul.

Hinduism

Hinduism is the dominant religion of the Indian subcontinent, and the third largest religion in the world after Christianity and Islam. Established over 3,000 years ago, Hinduism is based on ancient scriptures called the Vedas. Hindus believe in reincarnation through the cleansing of one's karma through a cycle of birth, death and rebirth.

Interconnectedness

Think of the unabashed stare that a baby has when seeing a new face; it has neither judgment nor friendliness—it is simply connecting with you as an extension of him or herself. Or think of the events of September 11, 2001—the implications rippled through our lives, reaching across the globe. Both of these examples illustrate our fundamentally interconnected nature.

Japa meditation

In Hinduism, this is the repetition of a mantra or divine name.

Karma

A Sanskrit word, this is the Hindu law of cause and effect. Often equated with our own expressions like "what goes around comes around," or "what goes up must come down," it must be considered in a much larger, spiritual context. Your actions and thoughts always have an impact on you and on the universe. Understanding this leads to seeing the value of compassion and generosity.

Logotherapy

This is a type of psychotherapy developed by Viktor Frankl. As described on the official Viktor Frankl Institute website, logotherapy's first principle is that humanity's primary motivation is the search for meaning. "Since persons are capable of deciding, they are also responsible for their decisions. A human being is not a mere puppet of biological, hereditary and environmental forces, but is always free to take a stand toward inner conditions and outer circumstances."

Lotus position

This is the classic cross-legged position used in yoga, also called Padmasana. Its benefits are that the spine is erect, the chest open and the flow of blood to the legs is constricted and redirected to the internal organs. It gets its name from the lotus flower, also called a water lily.

Lower self

The lower self encompasses the mind and the body, and defines *you* as only those two elements: a mind and a body. As such, it struggles to maintain your distance from others, and tells you that you must control, compete and criticize in order to survive. If given free rein, it can make your life a living hell.

Manifesting

Within the context of this book, to manifest is to bring events, people and moods into your life. It's something we all do every day, thanks to our attitudes, our awareness and our actions. But most of us aren't even aware of the fact that we have this power—we see life as something we must passively accept. To harness the power of manifesting is to bring it in line with your higher self. Use it—through meditation, compassion and mindfulness—to bring your deepest desires into your life, to create heaven on earth.

Mantra

A mantra is a series of syllables or words that is repeated during meditation. These words can be assigned by a guru, or can be selected individually.

It is commonly used in Buddhist meditative or ritual practices.

Mindfulness

To attain heaven on earth, it is important first to become aware of how the lower self infests itself into your daily life. Living in a state of mindfulness allows you to become fully aware of your choices, your moods and your actions. It is a kind of protection against the barrage of negativity that can be found in a given day, whether on television, at work, or in your own self-talk.

Namaste

Namaste is a virtually untranslatable Sanskrit word and gesture that embodies the connectedness that so many people find is missing in Western thought. It is uttered in greeting, and accompanied by pressing your own fingers against one another. Literally, the closest translation is "I bow to you." Physical contact—a handshake—is not required when you are connected spiritually to the person you meet, not to mention the universe.

Poverty consciousness

Poverty consciousness is a belief in limitation; it focuses your attention on what is lacking in your life. Like the proverbial half-empty glass, a person afflicted with poverty consciousness only sees what he or she is missing. It can refer to material things like money, clothes or cars, but can also include friends, love or family.

Quran

This is the Muslim holy book (also spelled Koran). It is believed to have been revealed to the prophet Muhammad during his life at Mecca and Medina in the seventh century C.E (according to the Western calendar).

Ramadan

Ramadan is the month-long celebration of Muhammad receiving the word of God and recording it in the Quran. It occurs in the ninth month of the Islamic calendar, and during that time Muslims must abstain from food and sexual intercourse from sunrise and sunset. It is at once a celebratory and a purifying period for Muslims.

Sanskrit

Sanskrit is considered one of the oldest written languages. Like Latin in Europe, it is still used in Hindu religious practices, though it is considered a dead language. Many Hindi ancient religious texts were recorded in Sanskrit.

Stoicism

This philosophical school was founded by Zeno in Cyprus around 300 B.C.E. Here is how the 2001 Columbia Encyclopedia describes it: "The universal working force, God, pervades all and becomes the reason and soul in the animate creation. In their ethical creed, the Stoics accepted virtue as the highest good in life. They identified virtue with happiness, claiming that it was untouched by changes in fortune. To live consistently with nature was a familiar maxim among the Stoics. Only by putting aside passion, unjust thoughts, and indulgence and by performing duty with the right disposition can people attain true freedom and rule as lords over their own lives."

Sufism

Sufism is a mystical branch of Islam that has a focus on seeing the unseen. Sufis have a parallel to the monks of early Christianity in their emphasis on asceticism and speaking directly with God. Rumi is perhaps the best known Sufi poet, dating back to the twelfth century C.E.

Unity consciousness

Like the cable that connects your computer to the Internet, unity consciousness is the thread that keeps the higher self energized. The higher self must be fueled by your awareness of your connection to others, to the universe and to the divine, in order to have power over the lower self. Meditation, silence and compassion are just some of the ways of "gassing up" your higher self.

Yogi

A yogi is someone who practices yoga, but generally refers to someone who has reached a spiritual plane higher than most through long-term yoga practice and meditation.

SUGGESTED READING

*T*HE FOLLOWING BOOKS HAVE HAD—AND still have—a profound impact on the way I look at the world. Sometimes all we need is one crisp, life-altering sentence or explanation that elevates our consciousness to a higher realm. Becoming wise is a process. To be more precise, becoming wise is a life-long process, with no ending. Just when you think you have it "all figured out," another book will come along and give you more words that open doors, dissolve barriers and broaden your perspective. The following books are must-reads for anyone committed to the ongoing search for wisdom. As you read these books you will begin to notice a number of universal truths or laws that appear and re-appear. As this transformation occurs, you will be seeing the world through the eyes of your higher self. The books below are listed alphabetically by title. Most of them have been quoted at least once in my book.

Bhagavad Gita
Available in various editions.

Written more than 2,500 years ago, the Bhagavad Gita or "Song of God" teaches the universal principles of spiritual warriorship, self-mastery and detachment through a story about a young warrior named Arjuna who is about to go to war. He has a conversation with the divine Krishna. Known as one of the world's great treasures, the Bhagavad Gita represents the holiest of Hindu philosophy and wisdom. Mahatma Gandhi used to read and recite the Gita every day. When asked why he read it, Gandhi said,

> When doubts haunt me, when disappointments stare me in the face and I see not a ray of light on the horizon, I turn to the Bhagavad Gita and find a verse to comfort me; and I immediately begin to smile in the midst of overwhelming sorrow.

Creating True Peace by Thich Nhat Hanh
(Free Press, 2003)

Every world leader should read this book. We all crave peace (internal peace and world peace), yet few ever seem to attain it. Hanh reminds us how compassion for one's self and others can transform suffering into enlightenment.

Culture of Fear by Barry Glassner
(Perseus Books Group, 1999)

This book will help you understand why everyone is so afraid of everything. It is filled with some pretty amazing insights into how the media manipulates the evening news by molding your perception of the world to fit their fascination with fear, horror and disaster. After reading this book, I decided to watch a lot less news and a lot less television in general.

Essential Sufism by James Fadiman and Robert Frager
(Castle Books, 1998)

This book, based on the teachings of Islam, reminds us that all real wisdom is already within us. It is filled with beautiful, ancient reminders of the one universal truth that we are all one.

How to Know God by Pantanjali
(Vedanta Press, 1996)

This is a book everyone must read, review and remember, for it is a book about who you are and your relationship to divinity. This is one of those rare books that change the way you see the world.

Meditations by Marcus Aurelius
Available in numerous editions; a recent translation is The Emperor's Handbook, translated by David Hicks and C. Scot Hicks (Scribner, 2002)

These truths written by the great Roman Emperor nearly 2,000 years ago will give you a heightened awareness of how to live life to the fullest. I have read and re-read this book at least a hundred times. The general theme is how to live in the moment.

Nothing is Impossible by Christopher Reeve
(Random House, 2002)

We know him as Superman. In real life he is more of a hero than any fictional character could ever be. In 1995, Chris had an accident while riding his horse, leaving him paralyzed. Read this book! It has heightened my gratitude for my mobility and served as a reminder of how fragile life is and how it can never be taken for granted. Truly inspirational.

The Only Dance There Is by Ram Dass
(Anchor, 1974)

Wow! Ram Dass is one of the great spiritual teachers. He is best known perhaps for his transformation from a Harvard and Stanford psychology professor to a philosopher and master storyteller. His sense of humor (and what a sense of humor he has) is peppered throughout the pages of this wonderful book. Ram shares great insights in this book on how to expand your awareness of who you really are.

The Power of Empathy by Arthur P. Ciaramicoli and Katherine Ketcham
(Dutton Books, 2000)

This book will help your communication skills go through the roof. It teaches us the incredible power of empathy and how to harness it to break down communication barriers to connect with others.

The Power of Now by Eckhart Tolle
(New World Library, 1999)

Everyone should read this book. Tolle reminds us, in his unique way, that all we really have is this moment. The book offers refreshing advice on how to spend less time worrying and more time living. And the only way to live is now.

The Power of Your Subconscious Mind by Joseph Murphy
(Simon and Schuster, 1963)

Murphy states, "Every thought is a cause and every condition is an effect." This book will teach you how the subconscious mind affects every decision you ever make. It will also teach you how to understand and program your subconscious mind to work for you rather than against you.

Power vs. Force by David R. Hawkins
(Hay House, 2002)

This book will give you a new understanding of the energy each thought creates and how it affects your life and everyone around you. The most intriguing concept of this book may be its explanation of consciousness and how to find the answers to any and all of your questions. Because the content of this book is so dense, I suggest reading it at least twice.

The Prophet by Kahlil Gibran
(Alfred A. Knopf, 1923)

The spiritual wisdom that Gibran weaves into this fictional masterpiece will reinforce the universal truths that will serve as your guide to living an extraordinary life.

There's a Spiritual Solution to Every Problem by Wayne W. Dyer
(HarperCollins, 2001)

Known as "the father of motivation," Wayne Dyer has been my mentor for the past two decades. This book will shed light on the many illusions that may be holding you back from connecting to your higher self.

Think and Grow Rich by Napoleon Hill
(Random House, 1937)

This classic is like an old friend to me. Mr. Hill wrote this book while working for President Roosevelt during the Great Depression. I can't think of any other book so full of advice on what to do and what not to do to create abundance in all facets of life.

Tuesdays with Morrie by Mitch Albom
(Doubleday, 1997)

I absolutely love this book! It is a true story about a dying teacher, Morrie Schwartz, and his many conversations about life with his former student. Morrie lovingly and honestly shares his regrets, lessons and advice about life.

Turning the Mind into an Ally by Sakyong Mipham Rinpoche
(Riverhead Books, 2003)

Sakyong refers to the mind as a wild horse that must be tamed to achieve true internal peace. This book is filled with ancient Buddhist insights and suggestions for achieving the self-mastery necessary to tame the wild horse. It is also a kind of how-to guide for meditation.

Walden by Henry David Thoreau
First published in 1854; various editions available.

I will admit that the book starts off on a bit of a windy road. I've heard people say that it is hard to read. It is, but every now and then he hits you with a sentence, paragraph or full page that is filled with so much wisdom that it is worth all the other pages where he goes on about how much money he spent building his house on Walden Pond (I believe it was $28.12).

INDEX

ABOUT THE AUTHOR

*D*ERRICK SWEET IS AN INTERNATIONALLY recognized speaker on "living life to the fullest," and founder of the Healthy Wealthy and Wise Corporation. Derrick travels extensively, speaking to leading corporations, government organizations and major associations (in support of their work-and-life balance programs, annual conferences and training and development workshops), sharing his insights about finding balance, creating internal peace and truly living life to the fullest.

Derrick is the author of *Get the Most Out of Life* as well as the highly acclaimed *Healthy Wealthy and Wise: The common sense guide to creating abundance in life.*

Prior to founding the Healthy Wealthy and Wise Corporation Derrick worked in the financial services industry. Before retiring at the age of thirty-eight, as Vice President and Senior Investment Advisor at one of the largest investment firms in Canada, Derrick managed approximately $60,000,000 on behalf of his clients in Canada, Ireland, Spain, Japan and Australia.

When Derrick isn't giving keynotes and workshops, he can be found expanding the company's Monthly Wisdom Program, a turn-key business franchise ideally suited for individuals who want to work part-time or full-time promoting the concept of living a full and complete life. For more information on the Monthly Wisdom Program please visit www.monthlywisdomprogram.com.

Derrick studied business at Johnson State College in Vermont, where he earned his Bachelor of Arts in Business Administration. Derrick lives at the Healthy Wealthy and Wise Lodge (nestled in the woods, in the Kawartha Lakes, Ontario) with his wife, Marsha, and their two Bouviers, Numan and Sadie.

To learn more about the Healthy Wealthy and Wise Corporation please visit healthywealthyandwise.com or call 416-410-9990.

Healthy Wealthy and Wise

The Healthy Wealthy and Wise Corporation has one purpose: to share the universal principles for creating abundance in your life. For over twenty years, author and speaker Derrick R. Sweet has researched the beliefs, actions and habits of some of the most successful people who have ever lived on our planet. The goal of Derrick's research was to go back thousands of years in search of the common link that consistently creates self-mastery. The "holy grail" of personal transformation that Derrick so enthusiastically shares is the same powerful tool that Buddha, Aristotle, Seneca, Albert Einstein, Thomas

Edison, and Abraham Lincoln embodied in their extraordinary lives.

In Derrick's keynote presentations and workshops, he not only focuses on what these actions and behaviors are, but reveals how to start applying them in your life today. Derrick also works one-on-one with individuals and team leaders from progressive corporations (on their goals, strategies, and mission statements) at the Healthy Wealthy and Wise Lodge in the Kawartha Lakes, Ontario. For more information please call 416-410-9990 or visit: www.healthywealthyandwise.com

Get the Most Out of Your Next Event!

Derrick Sweet is known as a truly gifted speaker. He speaks to leading companies, governments and associations internationally on what we can all do to live in the realm of our higher self. His hearty laugh, sense of humor, down-to-earth personality and raw enthusiasm for living life to the fullest have earned Derrick Sweet a reputation as one of the best keynote speakers in the world today.

Here's what people are saying about Derrick Sweet:

"Uplifting positive advice ... pay attention and grow."

—Dr. Wayne Dyer,
internationally bestselling author of
Your Erroneous Zones and *Your Sacred Self*

"Derrick Sweet's presentation to our teaching staff was motivational, inspirational, thought-provoking and butt-kicking—all at the same

time! His message was certainly enjoyable and uplifting, and his book, Get the Most Out of Life, is a must-read for all educators."

—Lou Vescio, Principal
A. N. Myer Secondary School
District School Board of Niagara

"It's obvious Derrick is getting the most out of life each day... and more. His energetic and positive approach to life shines through in both his inspirational presentations and his must-read books!"

—Carol Truemner,
Wellness Promotions Manager,
Sun Life Financial

"Awesome presentation! Loved it! Bring him back next year!"

—Human Resources Professionals
Association of Ontario

"Derrick Sweet is a truly wonderful individual; a positive outlook, humor and enthusiasm are of utmost importance in life and Derrick exudes these qualities in the presentation; his synergy with the participants is amazing! His integrity and authenticity are refreshing. His hands-on approach was simple to understand and easy to integrate into one's daily life. His ideas help us focus on our goals and develop a new way of seeing life."

—François Duguay,
Learning Centre Administrator,
Rogers Communications Inc.

"Your keynote presentation at our annual conference was inspirational to all in attendance! I heard many positive comments about your presentation. Your approach to group presentations gives us a fresh outlook on our lives! Thank you!"
—Amy Smithson,
Director of Education
West Virginia Credit Union League

"Derrick Sweet captivates his audience with his simplistic, common sense approach to enriching your everyday life! His laugh is infectious!"
—Sanyo Electronics